OLD ENOUGH

HOW 18-YEAR-OLDS WON THE VOTE
& WHY IT MATTERS

SHERI J. CAPLAN

Library of Congress Control Number: 2020914173

Caplan, Sheri J.

Old enough: how 18-year-old won the vote & why it matters / Sheri J. Caplan.

Pages cm.

Includes bibliographical references.

ISBN 978-1-7354930-0-8

Heath Hen

an imprint of Pettistripes LLC

Farmington, CT

www.heath-hen.com

Old Enough: How 18-Year-Old Won the Vote & Why it Matters/ Sheri J. Caplan.—1st ed.

ISBN: 978-1-7354930-0-08

WITH LOVE TO MOM, K, C, AND S

"Sitting this election out for whatever reason would not serve young voters' interest in the short or long term."

—*New York Times* Editorial Board, Apr. 12, 2020

CONTENTS

PREFACE

The more votes cast by youth the more likely is the politician to respond.

—William C. Mitchell

On the eve of ratification of the Twenty-Sixth Amendment, William C. Mitchell, a political science professor at the University of Oregon, wrote a slim book entitled *"Why Vote?"*. He aimed to encourage the country's new young voters to show up at the voting booth and to understand the significance of their ballots and encourage their involvement in public policy making.

This book shares those sentiments. Unlike Prof. Mitchell's book, it does not incorporate evaluative tools to assess candidates or utilize a social science framework. Instead, this book tells the often overlooked story underlying the origins and impact of the Twenty-Sixth Amendment by taking a quick romp through history while spotlighting various primary sources, popping in some images, and allowing for intermittent doses of wordplay, colloquialisms, popular culture references, and levity. By doing so, the book addresses a serious issue in a lighthearted way with the hope that maybe, just maybe, that approach might spur interest which will in turn spark greater voter participation.

That young people are typically thought to skew Democratic is not what motivated me to write this book. That notion, in fact, can prove fallacious. My hope is that Americans of all ages will exercise their right to vote throughout their lives. If this book helps motivate some to do so, and perhaps even foster a greater appreciation for learning about our history, it will have been worth the effort. That is why I wrote it.

Why does any of this matter? Because, as you no doubt have often heard, voting is the cornerstone of our democracy. But that cornerstone has harbored fault lines since the country was built. Increased stress now burdens our pillars of democracy, including the right to vote. Even without any glaring impediments, too many Americans, of all ages, often don't exercise this right.

In 1971, 18-year-olds gained the vote. The Twenty-Sixth Amendment, which gave them that right, was ratified in the shortest amount of time of any constitutional amendment. Like prior expansions of the franchise, wartime experience—both the Vietnam War and the cultural upheaval it caused—fueled the amendment's passage. Other cultural, societal, and political factors also figured into its acceptance. Its swift ratification belies not only a longer history of its origins but also a subsequent underwhelming voting turnout by young people.

Fast forward nearly fifty years. With the exception of the 2018 midterm elections, voter turnout among young voters remains disappointing. Various factors explain low voter turnout among young people. Youth themselves have been blamed for apathy and ignorance. More general societal influences include minimal civics education, uninspiring candidates, and uninterested campaigns. Other troubling issues include greater obstacles to voting that have been implemented in recent years by various states, some of which have a particular effect on younger voters, including onerous registration requirements and an absence of accessible polling places. The COVID-19 pandemic presents new challenges to in-person voting for everyone.

As Prof. Mitchell noted, elections are imperfect methods of communication and control. Still, to choose not to take part in them is to give up an important potential source of influence and participation, especially at a time when the country's democratic institutions and rule of law face pressure. By participating, you can strengthen them and the political process itself. If your preferred candidate isn't on the ballot or doesn't win, you will have still stepped forward to show that you care. Not voting only sends the message that you don't care. And if you don't care, others' views will be amplified and those might be very different from your own.

You may wonder, *"CAN A SINGLE VOTE MATTER?"*

Just ask Rutherford B. Hayes. In 1876, he won the presidency by one vote in the Electoral College. That one vote was cast by an Indiana delegate who had been elected to Congress by a one vote margin. A special commission subsequently charged with reviewing the Electoral College decision supported Hayes' election, again by just one vote.

Or ask John F. Kennedy. Nearly a century later, he beat Richard M. Nixon in the 1960 presidential election by 112,827 votes, a number essentially equivalent to one vote per precinct. He won twelve states by less than 1 percent of the vote.

And then, of course, the mere 327 vote margin in Florida during the 2000 presidential election led to the *Bush v. Gore* Supreme Court decision which effectively declared George W. Bush the winner.

"LET'S GET REAL," you say. Ok, in and of itself, it's unlikely your one vote might alter an election's outcome. But that scenario changes when others think the same way. Small variations can affect results. Use your influence to encourage others to vote. Show up on voting day. The difference begins with you.

This book does not advocate for a particular party or candidate. It simply touts what should be a non-partisan issue: voting strengthens our democracy and makes citizenship more meaningful. The very act of voting unites us even as we cast our ballots differently from each other.

THINK ABOUT IT...
PUT YOUR IDEALS INTO ACTION.
YOU ARE POWERFUL.
YOUR VOICE MATTERS.
REGISTER TO VOTE.
VOTE.
CONVINCE OTHERS TO VOTE.
CELEBRATE THE GIFT OF SUFFRAGE.

OUR COUNTRY NEEDS YOU.

ACKNOWLEDGMENTS

This book brings together various interests and areas of study of mine, including history, law, and civic life. None of those interests would have been fully realized without the wonderful education my parents made possible for me, both inside and outside the classroom. I treasure memories of political discussions with my late father and the excitement of voting for the first time.

The vast access to research materials on the internet made this project feasible. I hope others, particularly young people, take note of that and take advantage of available resources to delve deeper into topics raised in these pages or to explore their own interests.

I have no doubt that some may look askance at a treatment of a serious subject in a slightly unconventional way; i.e., some intentional digressions and irreverence interspersed into a factual and analytical commentary. Sorry, no apologies for that. History is not boring and need not be written that way.

This book also has a distinct point of view: citizens need to vote. This perspective should not be partisan or controversial, nor should its corollary, that formal or informal barriers to voting should not be tolerated. No apologies for those views, either.

This endeavor, much like my previous book, has been wholeheartedly encouraged and championed by friends and family, particularly by my mother, husband, and children. I could not have done this without their encouragement or that of the pets who have been by my side, and underfoot, every step of the way.

Once again, special recognition is due my husband, Dr. Kenneth A. Merkatz. He supported my intent from the outset to undertake this endeavor on a self-published basis so that I could retain control and allocate a portion of proceeds to non-partisan groups whose missions align with my perspective, as well as to offer a digital version on a pay-as-you-wish basis. He has served as this book's editor and spent hours polishing the manuscript, even while serving on the front lines during this pandemic. To the extent one finds merits in these pages, they can be attributed to his hand (which makes its appearance quite literally in a subsequent chapter), and to the extent one finds faults, they are mine.

Thank you all.

INTRODUCTION

Congratulations! You have turned 18!

You may get many presents in grand happy packages or in small joyful boxes.

They may all be awe-inspiring. Especially the one that jingles when you shake it.

(No, don't be expecting car keys).

NO PEEKING

You may lose what's inside of them. Or they may lose you. The trinkets will tarnish. The stylish frock will soon look frumpy. The electronics will fizzle and seem like yesteryear. And there certainly won't be anything left of the cake.

IT WAS A FINE CAKE

BUT THERE'S ONE GIFT THAT YOU'LL NEVER LOSE. OR OUTGROW. OR SMASH INTO THE CURB—LET'S NOT EVEN GO THERE.

YOU WILL ALWAYS HAVE IT. IT WILL TRAVEL WITH YOU ALONG LIFE'S JOURNEYS. AND YOU WILL CHERISH IT. BECAUSE IT IS LARGER THAN YOU. PEOPLE BEFORE YOU HAVE FOUGHT FOR IT AND CRIED FOR IT AND DANCED GREAT JOYS OF HAPPINESS FOR IT. NOW IT IS YOURS. EMBRACE IT.

ARE YOU READY? IS YOUR HEART POUNDING AND YOUR MIND RACING AND YOUR FINGERS TREMBLING?

HERE IS YOUR TICKET TO CHANGE THE WORLD. TO MAKE THE COUNTRY A BETTER PLACE. TO STAND UP AND SAY, "COUNT ME IN!"

HOORAY!
(NOTE TO SELF: REMEMBER TO REGISTER)

CONGRATULATIONS!! YOU CAN VOTE!

IT WASN'T ALWAYS SO.

18-YEAR-OLD AMERICANS COULD NOT VOTE UNTIL THE LATTER HALF OF THE 20TH CENTURY.

OVER THE YEARS, MANY FOLKS THOUGHT THEY SHOULD.

THIS IS THE STORY OF HOW **SHOULD** BECAME **COULD**,
AND WHETHER **COULD** BECAME **WOULD**.

I. SHOULD THEY?

EARLY AMERICA

TAKE ONE OF THOSE VIRTUAL REALITY GIZMOS YOU MAY HAVE AND DIAL IT BACK A FEW HUNDRED YEARS. THAT'S RIGHT, WE'RE NOW IN COLONIAL AMERICA. PUT AWAY YOUR PARTY HATS BECAUSE BIRTHDAYS THEN WEREN'T REGULARLY MARKED BY MUCH HOOPLA.

MANY HAPPY RETURNS, BEN!

Except for Ben Franklin. *Bon vivant* Ben had two birthdays thanks to a change in the calendar and family and friends celebrated on occasion by indulging in a plum pudding or hosting "a little dance." These events occurred when he was well into his senior years. As a boy, his special day (either of them) was likely spent much like any other.

Young people certainly made merry on occasion, but colonial life wasn't easy. At 14, white males often began apprenticeships that lasted seven years. A few lucky ones went to college. White females stayed home, practicing cooking, sewing, and the all-important task of goose-plucking.

A GOOSE

While these miniature adults performed many tasks vital to the functioning of the local economy and community, they couldn't vote.

MINIATURE ADULTS

Not until age 21. And then typically only if they were white, male, and of means. Some colonies also prohibited Catholics, Jews, and Quakers from voting.

Dawkins, Henry. *The election, a medley, humbly inscribed to Squire Lilliput, professor of scurrility*. Pennsylvania Philadelphia, 1764. (Library of Congress, Prints and Photographs Division).

That's because most colonies followed the British system that considered 21 to be the age of legal maturity for male subjects of the British Crown. (Massachusetts and New Hampshire briefly raised their voting ages to 24 in the late 1600s while boys under the age of 21 sometimes could vote in New England militia elections.)

What was magical about 21?

WELCOME TO ADULTHOOD

Well, at 21 a man could become eligible for knighthood in Britain. Although you only needed to be 20 to participate in political affairs in Ancient Greece, you might not have liked the whole toga thing.

TOGA! TOGA!

Money also mattered. Colonists echoed British notions that landowners and/or taxpayers merited a more serious stake in public affairs. This principle also solidified power in the hands of wealthy white men and denied it for others. In 1648, Margaret Brent, the first female property owner in Maryland and executor of Governor Leonard Calvert's estate, unsuccessfully petitioned the Maryland General Assembly for a vote.

> I've come to seek a voice in this assembly. And yet because I am a woman, forsooth I must stand idly by and not even have a voice in the framing of your laws.
>
> —MARGARET BRENT

Though when the colonists started getting uppity about British rule and complaining about lack of representation in affairs that affected them, they welcomed some of these others, including youth, to join their cause.

- 16-year-old Sybil Ludington rode forty miles in darkness to warn of approaching British forces.
- 16-year-old Peter Francisco, a Portuguese immigrant, joined the Continental Army and became known for his courage.
- 12-year-old Thomas Young served as a major in the militia.
- 16-year-old Peter Salem, a freed slave, became a hero at the Battle of Bunker Hill.
- 15-year-old Deborah Sampson disguised herself as a boy to join the military.

No one asked them to wait to participate in the country's affairs until their 21st birthdays.

But could they vote? **NO**

As much as the American Revolution was predicated on a fight for liberty and representation, the Founding Fathers did not regard the vote as a right of the masses. Taking pen to parchment, they expounded on their views.

Even Alexander Hamilton, himself an immigrant and a guy who liked very much to be in the room where it happened, didn't want to hold the door to that room open very widely. In 1775, he took to the social media of his era, the pamphlet, to set forth his perspective linking property to voting.

> **If it were probable, that every man would give his vote, freely, and without influence of any kind, then, upon the true theory and genuine principles of Liberty, every member of the community, however poor, should have a vote, in electing those delegates, to whose charge is committed the disposal of his property, his liberty and life. But since that can hardly be expected, in persons of indigent fortunes, or such as are under the immediate dominion of others, all popular states have been obliged to establish certain qualifications, whereby, some who are suspected to have no will of their own, are excluded from voting; in order, to set other individuals, whose wills may be supposed independent, more thoroughly upon a level with each other.**
>
> **—ALEXANDER HAMILTON**

John Adams shared sentiments similar to those of Hamilton. He also shared a life with Abigail, a feisty and erudite individual, and the duo appeared to be America's first power couple. Inside the Adams family, the two sometimes bickered over Abigail's festering concern with women's rights. After laughing off Abigail's suggestion in March 1776 that he

"Remember the Ladies" in the new code of laws being fashioned, John soon after wrote to a friend to espouse his view that men without property, women, and young people should not be entitled to vote.

... Such is the Frailty of the human Heart, that very few Men, who have no Property, have any Judgment of their own. They talk and vote as they are directed by Some Man of Property, who has attached their Minds to his Interest. . .

. . . What Reason Should there be, for excluding a Man of Twenty years, Eleven Months and twenty-seven days old, from a Vote when you admit one, who is twenty-one? The Reason is, you must fix upon Some Period in Life, when the Understanding and Will of men in general is fit to be trusted by the Public. Will not the Same Reason justify the State in fixing upon Some certain Quantity of Property, as a Qualification. . .

Depend upon it, sir, it is dangerous to open So fruitfull a Source of Controversy and Altercation, as would be opened by attempting to alter the Qualifications of Voters. There will be no End of it. New Claims will arise. Women will demand a Vote. Lads from 12 to 21 will think their Rights not enough attended to, and every Man, who has not a Farthing, will demand an equal Voice with any other in all Acts of State. It tends to confound and destroy all Distinctions, and prostrate all Ranks, to one common Levell.

—JOHN ADAMS

By the time of the Constitutional Convention in 1787, delegates believed in the importance of the vote yet still didn't consider many of their constituents important enough to merit it. At least when a wealth test was contemplated, Ben (Franklin, again) put a stop to that idea. He told his peers that "Some of the greatest rogues he was ever acquainted with, were the richest rogues." Later, he also considered the matter of property ownership and voting from a different perspective:

> Today a man owns a jackass worth fifty dollars and he is entitled to vote; but before the next election the jackass dies. The man in the mean time has become more experienced, his knowledge of the principles of government, and his acquaintance with mankind, are more extensive, and he is therefore better qualified to make a proper selection of rulers—but the jackass is dead and the man cannot vote. Now gentlemen, pray inform me, in whom is the right of suffrage? In the man or in the jackass?
>
> —BENJAMIN FRANKLIN

JACKASS

Jackasses aside, who did the Constitution as ratified in 1788 say could vote?

It didn't. Only 21 of the original Constitution's 4,400 words have anything to do with voting qualifications.

> the Electors [of U.S. Representatives] in each State shall have the Qualifications requisite for Electors of the most numerous Branch of the State Legislature.
>
> —U.S. CONSTITUTION, *Article I, Section 2*

Instead, the supreme law of the land punted on the issue of suffrage and kicked the matter back to the states to determine the breadth of the franchise within their borders.

So during the era when "We the people" formed a more perfect Union that rocked the world in ushering in a groundbreaking democratic framework, this very union was far from perfect. Although the Naturalization Act of 1790 permitted white men born outside of the United States to become citizens with the right to vote, Native Americans were not considered full citizens until 1924 (and it still took another forty years until all fifty states allowed them to vote). Many of the Founding Fathers owned slaves and slavery remained an issue that would eventually lead to civil war. The scourge of racial injustices continues into the twenty-first century. Basically, if you weren't a white male property owner, the new republic likely didn't include your ballot.

1800s–EARLY 1900s

IF YOUR IDEA OF THE 19TH CENTURY RELATES TO IMAGES OF VICTORIAN TEA PARTIES, THINK AGAIN.

CARE FOR TEA?

This era was anything but quaint. Westward expansion, Civil War, Reconstruction, industrialization, immigration. The country was changing at a rapid pace.

The right to vote also expanded.

At first, working class white males agitated for the vote. Savvy politicians recognized their potential clout, but various state efforts to abandon property requirements failed in the early years.

At the noisy New York State Constitutional Convention of 1821, future president Martin van Buren, who once asserted that he could not answer whether the sun rose in the East, threw some shade at those who sought to deny lower class suffrage. He clearly recognized that a broader electorate of white males could make the Democrats a powerful mass political party that might win the White House in the next election.

> And the question was, whether, in addition to those who might, by this Convention, be clothed with the right of suffrage, this class of men, composed of mechanics, professional men, and small landholders and constituting the bone, pith, and muscle of the population of the state should be excluded entirely from all representation in that branch of the legislature which had

> equal power to originate all bills, and a complete negative upon the passage of all laws; from which, under the present constitution, proceeded the power that had the bestowment of all offices, civil and military in the state; and above all, which, in the language of an honourable member from Albany, as a court of dernier resort, was entrusted with the life, liberty, and property of every one of our citizens.
>
> —MARTIN VAN BUREN

Chancellor of New York and legal scholar James Kent, famous for his equity jurisprudence, did not think equitable enfranchisement was prudent.

> That extreme democratic principle, when applied to the legislative and executive departments of government, has been regarded with terror, by the wise men of every age, because in every European republic, ancient and modern, in which it has been tried, it has terminated disastrously, and been productive of corruption, injustice, violence, and tyranny. And dare we flatter ourselves that we are a peculiar people, who can run the career of history, exempted from the passions which have disturbed and corrupted the rest of mankind? If we are like other races of men, with similar follies and vices, then I greatly fear that our posterity will have reason to deplore in sackcloth and ashes, the delusion of the day.
>
> —JAMES KENT

The New York convention ended with suffrage limited to taxpayers and to those serving in the militia. But by 1830, most states had abandoned property and income qualifications for adult white males to vote.

CAN A BOWL OF SOUP CHANGE HISTORY?

DEMOCRACY HAD BECOME TRENDY IN THE YOUNG REPUBLIC, AND NOTHING SAID DEMOCRACY MORE THAN TURTLE SOUP.

THE POOR DINED ON LEATHERBACKS CAUGHT IN THEIR YARDS AND THE RICH FEASTED AT TURTLE FROLICS. TURTLE WAS ON THE MENU WHEN JOHN ADAMS CELEBRATED VOTING FOR INDEPENDENCE, WHEN GEORGE WASHINGTON DINED WITH HIS OFFICERS IN A FAREWELL MEAL, AND WHEN ABE LINCOLN CELEBRATED HIS SECOND INAUGURAL THE NEXT CENTURY.

EVEN AARON BURR AND ALEXANDER HAMILTON SHARED A TASTE FOR TERRAPIN AS MEMBERS OF THE HOBOKEN TURTLE CLUB.

PERHAPS IF THEY HAD SLURPED UP A BOWL OF TURTLE SOUP TOGETHER IN THE WEE MORNING HOURS OF JULY 11, 1804, THINGS BETWEEN THEM MIGHT HAVE TURNED OUT DIFFERENTLY.

PARDONNEZ-MOI, MONSIEUR DE TOCQUEVILLE!
PERHAPS YOU ARE LOOKING FOR A TURTLE FÊTE?

BONJOUR, AMERICA!

Arriving on the scene in 1831, French aristocrat Alexis de Tocqueville toured the country to observe American society. Admittedly "baffled by the sheer quantity of food that people somehow stuff down their gullets," he assessed the American appetite for democracy.

When a nation modifies the elective qualification, it may easily be foreseen that sooner or later that qualification will be entirely abolished. There is no more invariable rule in the history of society: the further electoral rights are extended, the greater is the need of extending them; for after each concession the strength of the democracy increases, and its demands increase with its strength. The ambition of those who are below the appointed rate is irritated in exact proportion to the great number of those who are above it. The exception at last becomes the rule, concession follows concession, and no stop can be made short of universal suffrage.

—ALEXIS DE TOCQUEVILLE

EH, BIEN, ALEXIS, MAIS PAS TOUT À FAIT.

You were right about American eating habits but the path to universal suffrage not only halted, it faced obstacles, setbacks, and sometimes sputtered out. A few states abolished the right to vote they had once granted to freed Blacks and property-owning women. On the eve of the Civil War, property qualifications had disappeared for white males but many others, including Blacks, women, Native Americans, non-English speakers, and 18-21-year-olds still had to fight for their right to vote. Very often, that fight was built upon their patriotic service to the country. Wars provided the impetus for enlarging the franchise.

Even soldiers often faced obstacles to voting. The widespread absence of absentee ballots and incidents of voter suppression kept some otherwise enfranchised soldiers away from the ballot box during the presidential election of 1864.

> **If these volunteer citizen soldiers should not have a voice in the civil administration of the government for which they fight, then it would be well to inquire who is worthy of it. Though soldiers, they have not ceased to be citizens and residents, nor is their stake less in the country than that of those who remain in peace at home. Surely, he who stands faithfully by his country in the shock of battle may be safely trusted at the ballot box, though it should be carried to him at Vicksburg or Chattanooga.**
>
> **—MICHIGAN GOVERNOR AUSTIN BLAIR**

Blacks first had to be granted citizenship before they could vote. In 1857, the Supreme Court ruled in *Dred Scott v. Sandford* that Blacks could not be citizens. Ironically, outrage over that decision further polarized the North and South and pushed the country further down the path toward Civil War, in which Blacks' military service helped win their battle for citizenship.

Many free Blacks tried to enlist in the Union Army from the outset of the Civil War but were turned away. After Pres. Lincoln issued the Emancipation Proclamation, the government actively recruited Blacks to help meet their troop needs. Some Blacks were drafted by the 1863 Enrollment Act while others joined voluntarily, spurred on by the advocacy of Black leaders who understood the powerful argument for citizenship brought by military service.

> Once let the black man get upon his person the brass letter, U.S., let him get an eagle on his button, and a musket on his shoulder and bullets in his pocket, there is no power on earth that can deny that he has earned the right to citizenship.
>
> —FREDERICK DOUGLASS

By the time the Civil War ended on Apr. 18, 1865, over 186,000 Blacks in blue had played a vital role in securing the Union victory.

> I am for the "immediate, unconditional, and universal" enfranchisement of the black man, in every State in the Union. Without this, his liberty is a mockery; without this, you might as well almost retain the old name of slavery for his condition; for in fact, if he is not the slave of the individual master, he is the slave of society, and holds his liberty as a privilege, not as a right. He is at the mercy of the mob, and has no means of protecting himself.
>
> —FREDERICK DOUGLASS

Three constitutional amendments ratified during the Reconstruction era extended full citizenship rights to Blacks and represented the first real federal expansion of the right to vote. First, the Thirteenth Amendment abolished slavery. Next, the Fourteenth Amendment effectively overturned the dreadful *Dred Scott* decision by granting citizenship, due process, and equal protection of the law to all people born or naturalized in the United States. The Fourteenth Amendment said nothing affirmatively about voting rights. Instead, it included in its second section that representation shall be reduced if a state denies or abridges the right to vote to any male citizen age twenty-one and older, except for participation in rebellion or other crime. The fifth section explicitly gave Congress the power to enforce the amendment's provisions by appropriate legislation. Following advocacy by Blacks for the right to vote, the Fifteenth Amendment guaranteed Blacks the right to vote by prohibiting denial of the right to vote based on race.

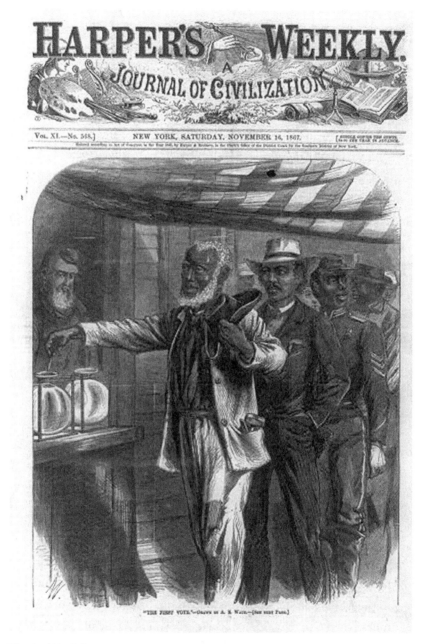

Waud, Alfred R., *The First Vote. Harper's Weekly*, v. 11, no. 568 (Nov. 16, 1867), (Library of Congress Prints and Photographs Division).

Immediately after Reconstruction, however, rampant voter suppression in the South, including poll taxes, literacy tests, fraud, and intimidation, impeded Blacks' right to vote.

They weren't the only group to find access to the ballot box blocked. Obstructionist tactics prevented many racial and ethnic minorities from voting. In addition, discriminatory laws targeted some groups explicitly. Asian American men faced restrictions stemming from the 1882 Chinese Exclusion Act that prevented individuals of Chinese descent from becoming citizens or voting. Native American men couldn't vote even if they paid taxes.

And no women could vote.

Since the Seneca Falls Convention in 1848, the demand for women's suffrage began to generate national interest. Beginning with the territory of Wyoming in 1869, a few Western states passed laws giving females the franchise, predominantly in order to woo more women to the frontiers. Nationally, the country remained reticent to grant women the vote. In 1872, Susan B. Anthony was arrested for casting an illegal ballot in the 1872 presidential election. During her trial the next year, she unsuccessfully invoked the Equal Protection Clause of the Fourteenth Amendment as entitling her to vote.

> **It was we the people-not we white male citizens-nor yet we male citizens-but we the whole people, who formed this Union; and we formed it, not to give the blessings of liberty, but to secure them-not to the half of ourselves and the half of our posterity, but to the whole people, women as well as men. And it is downright mockery to talk to women of their enjoyment of the blessings of liberty while they are denied the use of the only means of securing them provided by this democratic-republican government.**
>
> **—SUSAN B. ANTHONY**

Nevertheless, the suffragists persisted. They organized, advocated, and marched. It would take another war, World War I, to shine the spotlight on the hypocrisy between the American call for democracy and the denial of women's right to vote. Suffragists highlighted the contributions women made to the war effort.

The first picket line—College day in the picket line. Washington D.C., Feb. 1917. (Library of Congress Prints and Photographs Division).

In light of their arguments, political realities, and the noise outside the White House's windows, Pres. Woodrow Wilson finally endorsed female suffrage and supported the Nineteenth Amendment that was ratified in 1920.

> **We have made partners of the women in this war; shall we admit them only to a partnership of sacrifice and suffering and toil and not to a partnership of privilege and of right?**
>
> **—PRESIDENT WOODROW WILSON**

The American electorate essentially doubled.

If wartime contributions had helped Blacks and women win the vote, then youth might make that same argument. Since the eighteenth and nineteenth centuries, children sixteen and under often served in the military. Many youth under age 18 fought in the Civil War, despite higher draft ages in both the North and the South.

A few initiatives on the state level to lower the voting age had already appeared. In 1820, Missouri considered lowering the age but the proposal was overwhelmingly defeated. The next year, New York legislators rejected a similar proposal, but not after debating the idea for the first time that if a man was old enough to fight, he was old enough to vote. After the Civil War, several other state proposals to lower the voting age to 18 were considered but ultimately rejected.

In fact, the magical age of 21 seemed to gain significance through the Fourteenth Amendment. In the second section, aimed at penalizing states that did not permit Blacks to vote, the "right to vote" appears in the Constitution for the very first time by providing that 21-year-old male citizens must be allowed to vote or their representation would be proportionately reduced. That meant states could not set their voting age higher than 21.

(NOTE TO CLEVER READERS: NOTHING SAID THAT STATES COULD NOT SET THEIR VOTING AGE LOWER THAN 21.)

(ANOTHER NOTE TO CLEVER READERS: THIS SECTION IS ALSO THE ONLY PROVISION OF THE CONSTITUTION THAT EXPLICITLY DISCRIMINATES ON THE BASIS OF GENDER.)

Representatives shall be apportioned among the several States according to their respective numbers, counting the whole number of persons in each State, excluding Indians not taxed. But when the right to vote at any election for the choice of electors for President and Vice-President of the United States, Representatives in Congress, the Executive and Judicial officers of a State, or the members of the Legislature thereof, is denied to any of the male inhabitants of such State, being twenty-one years of age, and citizens of the United States, or in any way abridged, except for participation in rebellion, or other crime, the basis of representation therein shall be reduced in the proportion which the number of such male citizens shall bear to the whole number of male citizens twenty-one years of age in such State.

—U.S. CONSTITUTION, *14th Amendment, Section 2*

Flagg, James Montgomery, *I want you for U.S. Army: nearest recruiting station*. c. 1917. (Library of Congress Prints and Photographs Division).

During World War I, even Americans of voting age serving in the military overseas were effectively disenfranchised because no law for voting outside the United States then existed. Although the conflict slightly increased Congressional attention on extending the vote to those under 21 once the draft was extended to 18-year-olds shortly before the end of the war, opponents prevailed with arguments centering on the immaturity of youth.

Barney, Maginel Wright. *Follow the Pied Piper. Join the United States School Garden Army.* Washington, D.C; The Graphic Company, [1919?]. (Library of Congress Prints and Photographs Division).

Meanwhile, still younger Americans helped sell war bonds and enrolled in their own armies equipped with shovels and rakes. Despite the wartime contributions of America's youth, no vigorous seedlings of action to challenge the voting age took root.

1940s

WAR CHANGES EVERYTHING.
SOMETIMES THOSE CHANGES ARE PERMANENT.

Residents of New York's "Little Italy" in front of 76 Mulberry St., greet the news of the Japanese acceptance of Allied surrender terms with waving flags and a rain of paper. New York, 1945. (Library of Congress Prints and Photographs Division).

SOMETIMES NOT.

U.S. Office of War Information, Palmer, Alfred T. *Preparation for point rationing. Clearly posted cards indicating "ration points required" for various canned foods stacked on grocery shelves helps America's wartime marketers in using war ration book two.* Washington D.C, 1943. (Library of Congress Prints and Photographs Division).

SOMETIMES FOR THE BETTER.

Miller, J. Howard. *We Can Do It!* Office for Emergency Management. War Production Board. (01/1942-11/03/1945), (U.S. National Archives).

SOMETIMES FOR THE WORSE.

Lee, Russell. *Japanese-American evacuation from West Coast areas under U.S. Army war emergency order.* Apr. 1942. (Library of Congress Prints and Photographs Division).

One change occurred on the eve of World War II, in the decade's first year. It ushered in serious modern day consideration of the link between military service and the right to vote.

Miller, Chester Raymond. *Your right to vote...* U.S., ca. 1943. (Library of Congress Prints and Photographs Division).

On Sept. 16, 1940, Pres. Roosevelt enacted America's first peacetime draft. Two years later, during one of FDR's fireside chats (which actually occurred not in front of a cozy hearth but at a microphone-covered desk in the White House) he urged lowering the draft age from 21 to 18.

Harris & Ewing, photographer. *Franklin Delano Roosevelt Fireside Chat.* Washington D.C, Sept. 6, 1936. (Library of Congress Prints and Photographs Division).

Moving swiftly just five days after his urging, on Oct. 17, 1942 the House of Representatives voted on legislation doing just that. Little attention was paid to the issue of enfranchisement during the bill's consideration, though Rep. Lyle Boren (D-OK), that master of colorful language who two years before had called *The Grapes of Wrath* "a lie, a damnable lie" pointed out that teen manpower might not be needed if "swivel-chair soldiers" were engaged in active service. After he lamented that a million older volunteers had been rejected "by flatheads making rules against flatfeet," he pointedly referenced 18-and 19-year-olds.

> They are too young to vote, you say. Too young to fill the jobs in the factories and the offices, but you hold them to be old enough to die—old enough to face the hell of the battlefield. In God's name, what nonsense is this?
>
> —REP. LYLE BOREN (D-OK)

That same day, following a four hour floor debate that resulted in a broad margin of victory for lowering the draft age, Rep. Victor Wickersham (D-OK) introduced another age-based piece of legislation. He proposed a constitutional amendment to lower the federal voting age to 18.

He had not been the first to introduce such a proposal. In 1941, Sen. Harley Kilgore (D-WV) had offered a joint resolution that would lower the voting age to 18 by a constitutional amendment. No great interest in the idea had developed then and no action occurred, but American entry into World War II and a newly lowered draft age changed the dynamic.

> Mr. President, if young men are to be drafted at 18 years of age to fight for their Government, they ought to be entitled to vote at 18 years of age for the kind of government for which they are best satisfied to fight.
>
> —SEN. ARTHUR VANDENBERG (R-MI)

A few days following Rep. Wickersham's proposal, Sen. Arthur Vandenberg (R-MI) together with the legislator who became remembered for most ardently calling for lowering the voting age over the next three decades, Rep. Jennings Randolph (D-WV), offered companion legislative proposals that called for a Constitutional amendment to give 18-year-olds the vote.

Harris & Ewing, photographer. Rep. Jennings Randolph. Washington D.C, 1938. [or 1939] Photograph. (Library of Congress Prints and Photographs Division).

Drafted by legislative assistants, the text of Sen. Vandenberg's resolution eventually formed the crux of the 26th Amendment.

77th CONGRESS
2d Session

S. J. RES. 166

(Note.—Fill in all blank lines except those provided for the date and number of resolution.)

IN THE SENATE OF THE UNITED STATES

OCT 1 9 '42 LEG. DAY OCT 15 '42

Mr. VANDENBERG introduced the following joint resolution; which was read twice and referred to the Committee on *the Judiciary*

JOINT RESOLUTION

Proposing an amendment to the Constitution of the United States, *extending the right to vote to citizens 18 years of age or older.*

(Insert title of joint resolution here)

1   *Resolved by the Senate and House of Representatives of the United*

2   *States of America in Congress assembled*, (two-thirds of each House
concurring therein), That the following article is hereby
proposed as an amendment to the Constitution of the United
States, which shall be valid to all intents and purposes as
part of the Constitution when ratified by the legislatures
of three-fourths of the several States:

"Article 1

"Section 1. The right of citizens of the United
States, who are eighteen years of age or older, to vote
shall not be denied or abridged by the United States or by
any State on account of age. The Congress shall have power
to enforce this article by appropriate legislation.

"Sec. 2. This article shall be inoperative unless it
shall have been ratified as an amendment to the Constitution
by the legislatures of three-fourths of the several States
within seven years from the date of its submission to the
States by the Congress."

Senate Joint Resolution 166 Proposing the 26th Amendment, Oct. 19, 1942. (National Archives).

After the Teenage Draft Act became law on November 13, 1942, the injustice of forcing upon soldiers the burden to fight but not offering them the privilege to vote came into sharp focus.

Even the First Lady weighed in, though that should come as no surprise because Eleanor Roosevelt had a thing or two to say about many things. She had even written a children's book in 1932 (that only garnered a lukewarm review from the *New York Times*) about the importance of voting.

Eleanor Roosevelt votes in Hyde Park, New York, Nov. 3, 1936. (National Archives).

As if she didn't already have enough to do, what with holding press conferences, radio broadcasting, lecturing, and knitting incessantly for soldiers, Mrs. Roosevelt was the first First Lady (and so far, only) to pen a daily newspaper column. One day in "My Day" she wrote of her support for lowering the voting age.

I have noticed lately a number of articles in the papers, and even some cartoons on the subject, as to whether we should lower the voting age, since we have lowered the draft age. This question has been academically discussed for some time, but now it becomes more than an academic question.

If young men of eighteen and nineteen are old enough to be trained to fight their country's battles and to proceed from training to the battlefields, I think we must accept the fact that they are also old enough to know why we fight this war. If that is so, then they are old enough to take part in the political life of their country and to be full citizens with voting powers.

—ELEANOR ROOSEVELT

The National Education Association chimed in with its support. In an editorial in its trade journal, the NEA called for nonpartisan support and quick passage, citing the increased emphasis on social studies curriculums and the significance of high school.

One question lurked. If voting were linked to a military draft, what would happen if the draft age were ever lowered further? Should voting rights follow if 16-year-olds were subject to the draft? Not even the issue's champion thought so.

I feel there is a point below which we should not go.

—REP. RANDOLPH JENNINGS (D-WV)

Congress did not debate the topic of lowering the voting age. High schoolers did. To use the era's lingo, at a time when debate was a gas for eager beavers, aspiring orators found their killer diller topic.

RESOLVED:
18-Year Olds
Should Be
Allowed To
Vote

MOTION TABLED

Not all students thought lowering the voting age was a good idea. Nor did all adults. As critics pointed out, military service honed physical dexterity and subservience. Neither of those traits were required to cast a ballot.

Of all the crackpot things that have been taking place in recent years this is about the worst. How anybody can relate the capacity to tote a gun to experience in affairs of government is more than I can see.

—LETTER TO NEW YORK TIMES, AUG. 26, 1943.

Child welfare activist Dorothy Canfield Fisher echoed these sentiments, if not the same words. Concerned that a lower voting age might lead to removal of certain legal protections afforded young Americans, she wrote an article in the December edition for *Parent's Magazine* entitled "Raise Don't Lower the Voting Age."

Partisan politics figured little into the voting age issue. In Congress, Rep. Emanuel Celler (D-NY) and Sen. Richard Russell (D-GA) strongly opposed lowering the age despite some observers believing that youth leaned more Democratic. Even though overall public support grew for lowering the voting age to eighteen, no legislation moved forward.

Except in one state.

Under the hot Southern sun, the slogan "old enough to fight, old enough to vote" adorned pamphlets appearing in the Peach State and attracted support. In 1944, following a public referendum and sparked by the advocacy of Gov. Ellis Arnall, Georgia became the first state to lower its voting age to eighteen.

A PEACH OF A TOPIC

After World War II ended, pop culture began to focus less on politics

and more on pleasure. Attention drifted away from the voting age issue. One thing that caught the public eye was the emergence of a new kind of human species—**THE TEENAGER!!**

Although people had been advancing through the ages of 13-19 since time began, these creatures now possessed their own label. That wasn't trivial. Savvy marketers understood their budding economic impact, just as politicians later recognized their potential political significance. Notwithstanding a few concerns about hooliganism, for the most part teens were portrayed as innocent bobbysoxers who spent their time swooning over Ol' Blue Eyes and making scrapbooks, at least if you were a middle-class white girl.

SWOONATRA

As Americans be-bopped, the 1940s receded without voting age legislation advancing further. Yet those early days of the movement left their imprint.

The link between conscription and enfranchisement had been forcefully asserted.

The wording of the future amendment had been drafted.

The leading political proponent and foe had already appeared.

The public had considered and favored the issue.

All that needed to occur was a spark to reignite the conversation.

1950s

THAT SPARK TURNED OUT TO BE A BOOM.
IN FACT, SEVERAL BOOMS.
WAR.
ECONOMIC.
BABY.
ALL THREE IMPACTED THE VOTING AGE ISSUE.

The first boom was literal. The decade opened with hostilities breaking out on the Korean peninsula. In June 1950, the U.S. sent troops to Korea. Males between 18 1/2-26 were drafted to serve.

Once again, the unfairness of requiring young people to fight but not permitting them to vote came into focus.

In November 1952, the *Cleveland Plain Dealer* published Edward Kuekes's cartoon that showed two American soldiers during the Korean War carrying the body of a fallen solider on a stretcher. One asked, "Wonder if he voted?" and the other replies, "No, he wasn't old enough." The image won the Pulitzer Prize the following year.

New arguments in favor of lowering the age also emerged.

According to Sen. Blair Moody (D-MI) who testified at a 1952 Senate hearing on a proposed constitutional amendment to reduce the national voting age to 18, young people now were better educated and informed and capable of handling complex ideas.

> I remember reading of presidential elections in the past decided by such phrases as 'Tippecanoe and Tyler too' and the people around the country with the lack of communication systems never did realize the big issues.
>
> -Sen. Blair Moody (D-MI)

Although the one-day hearing may have tipped the balance in prompting the Judiciary Committee to favorably report on the measure in July, it did not rock the boat. The Senate took no further action.

Still, the refrain of a more engaged and capable younger generation reflected the growing optimism that Americans embraced. Who couldn't cheer a decade that brought the U.S. to the forefront of leadership on the global stage, and a bumper crop of babies on the home front?

BABY BOOM

As the byproducts of baby-making activity grew, these youngsters enjoyed greater access to education, technology, and information than ever before. In a culture of comfort, they attended a growing number of schools and came home to cookies and milk within the safety of nurturing families who could afford new tv sets and the latest toys. *GOLLY GEE! LIFE WAS FAB!* (At least that's how it appeared on *Leave it to Beaver*.)

GRAB YOUR TV DINNERS–IT'S THE CLEAVERS!!

Something else had also changed. The notion that young adults had political influence no longer seemed half-baked. Republicans now held power and young adults helped put them there. Nearly half of all voters under the age of thirty had backed Pres. Eisenhower in the 1952 election. The potential 6.3 million voters who would be added to the electorate if the minimum voting age were lowered to 18 could prove critical in a close presidential election.

In March 1953, four months before the Korean Armistice Agreement was signed, Sen. William Langer (R-ND) introduced Senate Joint Resolution 53, a proposal for a constitutional amendment that would make 18 the legal voting age in both state and federal elections. Both Pres. Eisenhower and Vice Pres. Nixon supported lowering the age.

When the Senate held a one-day hearing on the subject in June, however, three of the largest veterans' groups did not show up due to lack of interest. That didn't stop Ike from pitching the idea in his 1954 State of the Union address.

> **For years our citizens between the ages of 18 and 21 have, in time of peril, been summoned to fight for America. They should participate in the political process that produces this fateful summons. I urge Congress to propose to the States a constitutional amendment permitting citizens to vote when they reach the age of 18**
>
> **-PRESIDENT DWIGHT D. EISENHOWER**

Former Pres. Harry Truman did not agree.

> **Twenty-one is a better age; 24 would be better still.**
>
> **-FORMER PRESIDENT HARRY S. TRUMAN**

(Although "Give 'Em Hell Harry" claimed 18-year-olds did not have the knowledge to vote, he might have also been motivated to give a hard time to his successor. The Presidents' Club isn't always a comfy place. The two had been cordial until the 1952 election. By the time of planning for the 1953 inauguration, Ike worried "if I can stand sitting next to that guy.")

In any event, shortly after Pres. Eisenhower's urging, the Senate Judiciary Constitutional Amendments Subcommittee approved S.J. Res 53. A front page article in the *New York Times* on January 25, 1954 cited strong support in the Senate and among state governors for lowering the age, but did not think a constitutional amendment would likely get ratified.

Dwight D. Eisenhower takes the Oath of Office as President of the United States. Jan. 20, 1953. National Park Service. Identifier 68-352-1 (Dwight D. Eisenhower Library).

That's because other politicians thought the whole idea of 18-year-old voting stunk. Like cheese.

On March 10, the Big Cheese of the House Judiciary Committee, Rep. Celler, uttered one of the most delicious catchphrases of American legislative history:

Voting is as different from fighting as chalk is from cheese.

—Rep. Emanuel Celler (D-NY)

CHEESE. NOT CHALK.

As stinky as some may have found his objection, Rep. Celler's reasoning separated the whey from the curds.

> **If a person is too old to fight, is he too old to vote? Does the President mean that if a person votes, he must also fight? And does the President mean that girls must also fight? Many young men are unable to fight because they are physically unqualified to do so. Could it be that these men who cannot fight cannot vote?**
>
> **—REP. EMANUEL CELLER (D-NY)**

According to him, young people were more likely to:

- be amenable to indoctrination
- vote like ma and pa
- lose interest in elections after their first vote
- embrace extreme points of view due to their immaturity
- shun compromise

After invoking the specter of Hitler, Mussolini, and Stalin, each who had given teens the right to vote, Rep. Celler then introduced a bill proposing a constitutional amendment to prohibit any citizen under 21 from voting.

So much for the spirit of compromise.

Other opponents of lowering the voting age echoed these objections. But a fresh argument emerged that reflected another change in society, the beginning of the civil rights movement. In light of the recent Supreme Court decision on May 17, 1954 in *Brown v. Board of Education* that ruled school segregation unconstitutional, many Southern Democrats opposed a lower voting age on the grounds of infringement of states' rights.

These different perspectives converged one spring day. Despite Rep. Celler's refusal to hold hearings, S.J. Res 53 found its way to a vote on the Senate floor on May 21, 1954.

HAVE YOU EVER BEEN TO D.C. IN THE SPRING?

IT'S A LOVELY PLACE. ESPECIALLY IN APRIL WHEN THE CHERRY BLOSSOMS DAZZLE.

But on May 21, it was hot, hot, hot. Late that Friday afternoon, the Senators took up debate. They might have been dreaming of leaving for the shore but inside the Senate chamber, it was no day at the beach.

SENATE CLOCK STRIKES 4:00

Maybe it was the heat that produced some memorable remarks as the Senators sparred. After Sen. William Langer (R-ND) opened the debate by invoking Ike's support, he reiterated the draft argument and the fact that 18 was considered the age of maturity in many other civil contexts. He also spoke about recently visiting the set of a *Youth Wants to Know* television show, whereupon the young people's savvy impressed him.

(IMAGINE IF HE HAD INSTEAD WATCHED REBEL WITHOUT A CAUSE THAT HAD BEEN RELEASED A YEAR EARLIER...)

> **When I left that television studio, I was more firmly convinced than ever than an 18-year-old should have the right to vote.**
>
> **—SEN. WILLIAM LANGER (R-ND)**

Sen. Richard Russell (D-GA), who ironically hailed from the only state that then permitted teen voting, advocated against the measure by invoking states' rights.

> I do not propose to vote to coerce any other State of the Union to follow the example of my State.
>
> —SEN. RICHARD RUSSELL (D-GA)

Countering that argument, Sen. Everett M. Dirksen (R-IL) pointed out that the ratification process itself relied upon state preferences. He further reminded his peers that voting is not compulsory.

> If you are interested enough and if you have the intelligence and the capacity to discharge the responsibility as a part of the American electorate, then march yourselves to the polls and vote. If you do not want to go there, it is all right; it is deplorable, but it is still all right, because under the laws of the United States there is nothing to compel a young man or young woman to go to town and mark a ballot.
>
> —SEN. EVERETT M. DIRKSEN (R-IL)

A youthful 37-year-old Sen. John F. Kennedy (D-MA) chimed in, citing brevity of hearings and lack of state actions.

> **Therefore, although the maturity and wisdom of those in this age group is not to be deprecated-indeed, I would support such an amendment in my own State, and in the Congress if it were supported by the experience and demand of many States-there have not been demonstrated sufficient grounds for changing this basic document today.**
>
> **—Sen. John F. Kennedy (D-MA)**

His even younger peer, 35-year-old Sen. Russell Long (D-LA) who made a point of referencing his status as the youngest Senator, voiced his opposition on grounds of states' rights, insufficient hearings, and his opinion that 21 represented a more mature and better qualified electorate.

> **I am entirely convinced that there are a great many 18-year-olds in every State in the Union who are well qualified to vote; I am likewise convinced that every one of those young people would be even better qualified if they were to wait until they are 21 before casting their first ballot.**
>
> **—Sen. Russell Long**

Ultimately, after two hours of banter, some witty, some otherwise, the bill fell five votes short of approval. Republicans unanimously voted in favor of the proposal while Democrats split their votes. The *New York Times* attributed the defeat in part due to "poor planning" of timing the vote on a "getaway day."

SEE YA'

Other places did get it together.

In 1954, the territory of Guam lowered its voting age to 18. Kentucky ratified a constitutional amendment to lower its state voting age to eighteen in November 1955.

Three years later, the territory of Hawaii sets 20 as its minimum voting age.

Alaska followed suit, stipulating 19 as the minimum voting age in its constitution that took effect upon its admission as a state in 1959. Three years earlier, the Last Frontier had hammered out its governing document at a constitutional convention. At the opening of proceedings, Gloria Fredericks, the student body president of Nenana Public Schools, addressed the delegates by countering the country's concerns over juvenile delinquency.

> I feel that today's youth are more alert, more self-conscious, and more capable than the youth of any other nation in the entire world. Were we to doubt our advancement over other generations, we wouldn't admit the failure of our great American principles. We, the youth of 1956, are indeed alert to the changes of our day.
>
> —GLORIA FREDERICKS

While Fredericks may have felt assured of her generation's capabilities, the public harbored growing concerns about youth. By the late Fifties, the same teenagers who had previously been lauded as enlightened were now characterized as reckless and subversive.

Why?

COMIC BOOKS.

In 1953, the Senate established a subcommittee to investigate rising juvenile delinquency. Comic books became the focus of hearings the following year.

> **This country cannot afford the calculated risk involved in feeding its children, through comic books, a concentrated diet of crime, horror, and violence.**
>
> —INTERIM REPORT OF THE COMMITTEE ON THE JUDICIARY, 1955–56

PANTY RAIDS.

Having tired of goldfish swallowing contests, college males moved on to a new form of entertainment—raiding female dorms in a quest for undergarments. This did not impress one Georgia lawmaker who observed that "the recent series of panty raids has not inspired much confidence in the judgment of college students."

ELVIS.

A new kind of music, rock 'n roll, took over the airwaves and began to get teens all shook up. When the Maryland legislature considered 18-year-old voting in 1957, one state senator noted that most Elvis fans were young and asked, "Do you think that's a proper frame of mind for voters?"

QUITE FRANKLY, TEENS WERE STARTING TO SCARE THE HECK OUT OF ADULTS.

Whether or not teens were going to hot rod straight to the jailhouse, plenty of things in Fifties society weren't quite as perfect as *Leave it to Beaver* portrayed. These things were more significant than teens talking back to their parents.

A culture of apparent conformity belied rising discontent. Deep fissures in society lurked beneath the model homes of suburbia and southern city streets.

They erupted following the 1954 Supreme Court decision in *Brown v. Board of Education* that held racial segregation in schools unconstitutional.

Southern politicians devised a campaign of "Massive Resistance" to desegregation. Violence against Blacks also rose. Fourteen-year-old Emmett Till was brutally murdered in August 1955 after allegedly offending a white woman. His killers were acquitted.

The nation could no longer look away from the nascent civil rights movement.

Rosa Parks, a 42-year-old Black seamstress, chose non-violence. Like 15-year-old Black high school student Claudette Colvin had done nine months earlier, Parks refused to give up her seat on a Montgomery, Alabama city bus to a white passenger in December 1955. Her insistence on sitting down inspired others to stand up and to boycott city buses for a year in what is considered the first large-scale American demonstration against segregation.

On the third anniversary of *Brown*, national civil rights leaders led a march in Washington, D.C. to encourage the federal government to work toward implementing the ruling. There, on the steps of the Lincoln Memorial, Dr. Martin Luther King, Jr. exhorted both political parties to ensure voting rights of Blacks.

Give us the ballot, and we will no longer have to worry the federal government about our basic rights.

Give us the ballot, and we will no longer plead to the federal government for passage of an anti-lynching law; we will by the power of our vote write the law on the stature books of the South and bring an end to the dastardly acts of the hooded perpetrators of violence.

> Give us the ballot, and we will transform the salient misdeeds of bloodthirsty mobs into the calculated good deeds of orderly citizens.
>
> Give us the ballot and we will fill our legislative halls with men of good will and send to the sacred halls of Congress men who will not sign a "Southern Manifesto" because of their devotion to the manifesto of justice.
>
> Give us the ballot, and we will place judges on the benches of the South who will do justly and love mercy, and we will place at the head of the southern states governors who will, who have felt not only the tang of the human, but the glow of the Divine.
>
> Give us the ballot, and we will quietly and nonviolently, without rancor or bitterness, implement the Supreme Court's decision of May seventeenth, 1954.
>
> —DR. MARTIN LUTHER KING, JR.

In early September, nine Black students attempting to attend Little Rock Central High School faced an angry mob as well as the Arkansas National Guard who had been deployed by the state's governor to block them from entry. By the end of the month, Pres. Eisenhower sent federal troops to escort and protect the group that had become known as the Little Rock Nine. Despite their admittance to the school, they faced continued hostilities while public resistance to school desegregation continued.

Bledsoe, John T, photographer. *Mob marching from capitol to Central High.* Little Rock, Arkansas, 1959. (Library of Congress Prints and Photographs Division).

On September 9, 1957, five days after the initial attempt made to integrate Little Rock Central High School, Pres. Eisenhower signed the Civil Rights Act of 1957 into law, the first federal civil rights legislation since Reconstruction. Among its provisions, in an attempt to curtail discriminatory voter registration rules and other barriers to voting that many Blacks encountered in the South, the law prohibited interference with a citizen's right to vote and empowered the Justice Dept. to monitor abuses.

Meanwhile, the situation in Vietnam was building toward a showdown. In May 1954, Pres. Eisenhower outlined his administration's "domino theory" that asserted the fall of Indochina to the Communists would lead to the rapid collapse of other democratic nations. He used this rationale to justify increasing American involvement in the conflict.

DOMINO THEORY

But this game theory did not end the question of lowering the voting age.

No showdown occurred on 18-year-old enfranchisement.

No falling domino knocked off a quick race to give young people the ballot.

Through the first half of the Fifties, the voting age issue bopped along, gyrating the most excitement with the Senate vote in 1954. This was the farthest it had ever gotten. Afterwards, the subject did little on the federal level but spin around. As the decade wound down, teens may have been all shook up but it didn't look like they would be gaining the vote anytime soon.

1960s

IF THE FIFTIES CELEBRATED CONVENTIONALITY, THE SIXTIES REVELED IN UPROOTING THE STATUS QUO.

Civil rights advanced, environmental activism took root, a new wave of feminism emerged, the modern gay rights movement accelerated, Native American concerns received greater federal attention, and the beginning of the end of the Vietnam War came into sight.

Conflict engulfed America. But the nation's youth were not conflicted—they wanted change. No longer branded as mischievous hooligans, they were now seen by many as dangerous radicals who ignited and fanned the flames of political activism. The lingering problems of racial inequality and the Cold War particularly caught their attention, more so even than their own quest for a lowered voting age. Ironically, both issues catalyzed subsequent progress toward lowering the voting age.

In the first few months of 1960 alone, young people stood at the forefront of change:

- Students for a Democratic Society, the newly named radical student activist group that became the most notable student political organization of the counterculture era, first met in Ann Arbor, MI.

- Four Black college freshmen sat at a whites-only counter at Woolworth's in Greensboro, North Carolina and refused to leave until served.

- The Student Nonviolent Coordinating Committee (SNCC) formed as an interracial group promoting civil rights reforms advocating non-violence.

And this was only the start to the most tumultuous decade yet in U.S. history. (ALTHOUGH THE BEGINNING OF THE 2020s LOOKS OMINOUS.)

In November, 43-year-old Sen. Kennedy emerged victorious in the only presidential election that ever pitted two candidates under the age of 50 against each other. Winning with the slimmest of margins but the more telegenic appearance, he garnered the support of 54% of voters under thirty.

When JFK asked in his inaugural speech what you could do for your country, this new generation had answers.

They organized, advocated, and marched to protest segregation. Even the youngest among them took part. In November, 1960, six-year-old Ruby Bridges, escorted by federal marshals needed to keep an angry mob at bay, desegregated her previously all-white local elementary school in New Orleans. In May, 1963, more than 1,000 students from first graders to high school seniors faced arrest and police armed with water hoses, batons, and police dogs as they marched out of their classes in Birmingham, Alabama to protest the city's segregation.

And they registered voters.

Central to the civil rights movement was securing voting rights. Blacks still faced obstacles and even violence when they went to the polls.

Young Americans marched on Washington, volunteered for the voter registration project in Mississippi known as Freedom Summer, and crossed the bridge across the Alabama River in Selma to demand that Blacks be allowed to exercise their constitutional right to vote. They faced bigotry, violence, and worse. Three young voting activists were murdered.

> **The first time I was arrested was in September of 1963. I was carrying a sign that said "ONE MAN, ONE VOTE." For that I was arrested and taken to jail.**
>
> **—JOHN LEWIS**

Trikosko, Marion S. Photograph, *John Lewis speaking at a meeting on American Society of Newspaper Editors*, Statler Hilton Hotel, Washington, D.C., Apr. 16, 1964. (Library of Congress Prints and Photographs Division).

While youth powered voter registration efforts aimed to empower others, their own route to the ballot box languished during the first half of the decade. Although the Trust Territories of the Pacific set its voting age at 18 in 1964 and American Samoa lowered its age from 20 to 18 in 1965, most states voted down similar proposals. Democrats enjoyed an edge with younger voters again in the presidential election of 1964, but the party's southern contingent still cited concerns over states' rights and increasing federalization of voting rights to resist lowering the age.

Still, the voting age issue cropped up from time to time. When Congress had debated enabling legislation in 1961 for the Twenty-Third Amendment that gave District of Columbia residents the right to vote in presidential elections, both the Kennedy Administration and Sen. Estes Kefauver (D-TN) advocated for 18 as the requisite age, citing advances in education, communications, youth interest in public affairs, and longevity. To no such avail, 21 prevailed.

Undeterred, Sen. Kefauver held hearings that year on lowering the age to 18 but no proposal moved forward. Other efforts to broaden the franchise did.

In 1962, Congress passed the Twenty-Fourth Amendment that prohibited poll taxes in federal elections. The amendment was ratified in January 1964.

On August 28, 1963, about a quarter million people participated in the March on Washington for Jobs and Freedom that called for the civil and economic rights of Blacks. On the steps of the Lincoln Memorial, Dr. King told the crowd about his dream. Voting rights figured prominently in his vision.

Now is the time to make real the promises of democracy. . .

There will be neither rest nor tranquility in America until the Negro is granted his citizenship rights. . .

We cannot be satisfied as long as the Negro in Mississippi cannot vote and the Negro in New York believes he has nothing for which to vote.

—MARTIN LUTHER KING, JR.

At the same time that efforts to guarantee voting rights for those blocked from access were gaining momentum, there emerged a documented recognition that many other Americans simply didn't bother to exercise their right. In December 1963, the President's Commission on Registration and Voter Participation, born out of concern that one-third of adults did not vote in presidential elections, issued "standards," including lowering the voting age.

Voting by Persons 18 Years of Age Should Be Considered by the States

—STANDARD XVI

The report suggested voter registration days at high schools and that states incorporate into their curriculum a three-point action plan to inspire good citizenship in high school seniors:

1. Explanation of the importance of a single vote to the American way of life.

2. Information on the requirements and mechanics of registration.

3. Demonstration of the actual process of voting in the local community.

But even an A in citizenship could equate to an F in voting because high school students could only obtain a ballot three years after they received a diploma. The report attributed low voter turnout among young Americans to growing disinterest in public affairs after graduation.

According to the report, some young people might be lost as voters for the rest of their lives.

For Blacks, low voter turnout had less to do with political disinterest than with obstacles to voting that persisted despite the 1964 ratification of the Twenty-Fourth Amendment that prohibited poll taxes. With the '64 presidential election looming and the Civil Rights Act of 1964 facing opposition in the Senate, Malcolm X delivered a powerful speech, excoriating politicians and gerrymandering, where he called upon the Black community to use the ballot like a weapon to achieve change.

> **We suffer political oppression, economic exploitation and social degradation...**
>
> **So today our people are disillusioned. They've become disenchanted. They've become dissatisfied. And in their frustrations they want action And in 1964 you'll see this young black man, this new generation, asking for the ballot or the bullet.**
>
> **—MALCOLM X**

The murder of civil rights activist Jimmie Lee Jackson when unarmed and participating in a voting rights march in Alabama in February 1965 and other violence helped inspire the Selma to Montgomery marches in which protestors demonstrated for protection of the constitutional right to vote. Again, the non-violence protest was met with violence.

Bloody Sunday officers await demonstrators, 1965, Selma, Alabama (U.S. Dept. of Justice).

During the first march that took place on March 7, 1965, later known as Bloody Sunday, state troopers and others attacked unarmed marchers with tear gas and clubs. SNCC Chairman John Lewis suffered a skull fracture. Two days later, on the evening of the second march, civil rights activist James Reeb who had come to participate was murdered. Federal protection of the protestors did not occur until the third demonstration, held on Mar. 21.

I don't know how President Johnson can send troops to Vietnam, but he can't send troops to protect people in this country who only want to register and vote.

—John Lewis

(reflecting in 2014 on the struggle for passage of the Voting Rights Act)

On Mar. 15, Pres. Lyndon B. Johnson addressed Congress in a nationally televised session to request a new federal voting rights law.

> There is no constitutional issue here. The command of the Constitution is plain.
>
> There is no moral issue. It is wrong—deadly wrong—to deny any of your fellow Americans the right to vote in this country. There is no issue of States rights or national rights. There is only the struggle for human rights.
>
> —PRESIDENT LYNDON B. JOHNSON

In August, 1965, the landmark Voting Rights Act of 1965 that banned racial discrimination in voting, including both formal and informal barriers, became law.

> If you do this [register and vote], then you will find, as others have found before you, that the vote is the most powerful instrument ever devised by man for breaking down injustice and destroying the terrible walls which imprison men because they are different from other men.
>
> —PRESIDENT LYNDON B. JOHNSON

Pres. Johnson had considered including a provision in the draft Voting Rights Act legislation that would have lowered the voting age to 18. The linkage of lowering the voting age to broadening the franchise could not have been more explicit had he done so. But he didn't.

BLUEBONNETS (NEAR LBJ RANCH)

Down home on his ranch where bluebonnets bloomed, LBJ noted he had been advised that lowering the age would have needed a constitutional amendment.

A DUCK (NEAR HARVARD)

Up in his ivory tower, blueblood Harvard Law Prof. Archibald Cox argued otherwise in an article in the *Harvard Law Review* published the following year. He believed Congress could reduce the age simply by statute.

Across America meanwhile, while less and less actual legislation advanced to lower the voting age, more and more young people were seeing action.

TO BATTLE

In August, 1964, the Gulf of Tonkin Resolution authorized the president to use military force in Southeast Asia. By the end of 1965, over 200,000 Marines had been sent to Vietnam. More than 300,000 young men received draft notices in 1967.

In May of that same year, 64% of Americans, the highest percentage ever, favored lowering the voting age to 18. Once again, the factor igniting greater support for lowering the voting age seemed to be war. But this time, the war itself was causing fissures in society rather than uniting the country.

THE TIMES, THEY WERE A' CHANGIN'.

Amid a flourishing counterculture, support for the war quickly eroded.

Thousands of Americans from all walks of life demonstrated against the war. An anti-establishment generational divide emerged as young folks figured prominently in the protests. Co-eds staged sit-ins on college campuses, yippees burned draft cards in city streets, and hippies turned on, tuned in, and dropped out all over the country.

SIGNS OF THE TIMES

Young folks no longer seemed adorably mischievous or even a bit unruly— they were upending the social order and alarming their elders.

And that was all before the most unforgettable year in American history, 1968— a year in which 15-year-olds won the vote and elected a 24-year-old rock star as president who then imprisoned all adults over age 35 and forced them to wear purple robes and ingest LSD.

"WILD IN THE STREETS"

OK, SO THAT REALLY WAS A HORROR SHOW.

Or, in the words of a *New York Times* critic who deemed it "By far, the best American film so far," *Wild in the Streets* represented "a very blunt, bitter, head-on but live and funny attack on the problem of the generations." The paper referenced the movie again in 2016, this time referring to it as "an artifact of 1968" but one nonetheless whose "image of generational megalomania provides an ominous footnote to the current presidential election, which could be the last to be waged by two baby boomers."

(WELL, NOT QUITE. ELECTION 2020 IS SHAPING UP TO BE A CONTEST BETWEEN TWO SEPTUAGENARIANS—ONE CANDIDATE BORN AT THE END OF THE SILENT GENERATION AND THE OTHER BORN AT THE BEGINNING OF THE BABY BOOM GENERATION.)

SOME THINGS THAT <u>REALLY DID</u> HAPPEN IN 1968

- JANUARY: North Korea captures USS Pueblo
- Tet Offensive
- FEBRUARY: Memphis sanitation workers killed
- Orangeburg Massacre
- Kerner Commission Report finds 1967 riots a result of racial economic inequality
- MARCH: Latino high school students in Los Angeles walk out to demand improved education
- Howard University students stage sit-in for greater voice in school matters
- My Lai Massacre
- APRIL: MLK assassinated; riots ensue in 100 cities nationwide
- Fair Housing Act signed
- Columbia University sit-in demanding end to military research
- MAY: Louisville Riots
- Catonsville Nine
- JUNE: RFK assassinated
- Poor People's Campaign holds Solidarity Day Rally in D.C.
- JULY: UC Glenville shootout
- AUGUST: DNC protests
- SEPTEMBER: Miss America protest

- OCTOBER: Mexico '68 Olympics
- Apollo 7 broadcasts
- NOVEMBER: Nixon elected with .7% popular vote margin
- Shirley Chisholm elected first Black woman representative
- *Star Trek* airs first televised interracial kiss
- "National Turn in Your Draft Card Day
- DECEMBER: Apollo 8 first manned spacecraft orbits the moon

Despite young folks terrifying their elders both at the box office and really most everywhere, the voting age issue took on renewed gravity that year.

Politicians noted that the baby boom would soon lead to burgeoning ranks of Americans between 18 and 34. The sheer energy and potential impact of an engaged youthful political base showed itself in the presidential campaign of Sen. Eugene McCarthy (D- MN). Thousands of college students "got clean for Gene" as they cut their hair and shaved to put in a clean-cut appearance for their anti-war candidate. McCarthy lost the nomination but won the envy of his peers over his legions of young volunteers.

PRE-GENE/CLEAN FOR GENE

Not all young folks cleaned up their acts. Amid 150 violent campus demonstrations occurring throughout the nation between 1968-69, concern over student radicalism spilled across partisan lines. Politicians from both parties argued for the need to harness young political energy.

Could the ballot lessen the tension?

In May 1968, a record high 64% of Americans supported lowering the voting age. At Senate hearings, a proposed constitutional amendment to lower the age seemed "to have more punch than previously," with growing bipartisan support.

> This force, this energy, is going to continue to build and grow. The only question is whether we should ignore it, perhaps leaving this energy to dam up and burst and follow less-than-wholesome channels, or whether we should let this force be utilized by society through the pressure valve of the franchise.
>
> —SEN. BIRCH BAYH (D-IN)

> I am convinced that self-styled student leaders who urge such acts of civil disobedience would find themselves with little or no support if students were given a more meaningful role in the electoral process.
>
> —SEN. JACOB JAVITS (R-NY)

> Many older people yearn for the good old days of the 1950's when gray-flanneled youth declined to be identified with civic issues lest the corporate recruiters would regard overactive participation as a blemish on student records. I favored the

> 18-year-old vote then in order to blast some students out of their indifference. Today, the 18-year-old vote is needed to harness the energy of young people and direct it into useful and constructive channels, not simply for their benefit, but for the benefit of the entire Nation.
>
> —REP. KEN HECHLER (D-WV)

In June, Pres. Johnson submitted to Congress a proposal for a constitutional amendment to lower the voting age to 18.

> [It is a signal] to our young people that they are respected, that they are trusted . . . and that the day is soon to come when they are to be participants, not just spectators, in the adventure of self-government.
>
> —PRESIDENT LYNDON B. JOHNSON

A few days later, the *New York Times* reversed its past opposition.

> In a real sense, of course, there is no magic date on which people become 'old enough' to vote. Some never have the maturity to make an intelligent contribution to public affairs, regardless of what the calendar says. . .
>
> More than half the national population will soon be under 25 years of age. There is already an over-ready disposition on the part of many of these young people to tune out of the society—to decide without any real trial that there is no hope for effecting change through the political process.

> **This escapist trend will be less assertive if more youth have an opportunity to participate directly in the selection of public officials and the shaping of public policies. It is chiefly for that reason that we believe, despite our previously expressed views to the contrary, that the good of the nation as well as its youth will be served if extension of the franchise channels this potent reservoir of fresh perception and idealism into the often stagnant mainstream of American political life.**
>
> *-New York Times*

The legislative clock ran out on Pres. Johnson's proposal but the idea remained. Despite some concerns that young people might be subverted by alien influences or the intrusion of political parties onto college campuses, the 1968 Democratic party platform supported a constitutional amendment to lower the voting age to 18 and the Republican platform called on the states to reevaluate their voting age minimums.

Richard M. Nixon won the 1968 election while capturing only 38% of the vote of those under 30 despite his support for 18-year-old voting. But the ballot now no longer became cast only as a reward for service or as an entitlement but as an antidote to unrest.

ELECTION ELIXIR

> **Once our young people can sound off at the polls, I believe there will be less need to sound off in the streets.**
>
> —VICE PRESIDENT SPIRO AGNEW

The fear of student radicalism gave strength to the lowered voting age movement. Students themselves increasingly organized at a grassroots level. Some found LUV.

Responding to a speech made by Sen. Bayh on the University of Pacific campus in December 1968 in which he challenged students to pressure Congress to lower the voting age, students established LUV (Let Us Vote) that gave rise to 207 college and 1500 high school chapters just three weeks later. They joined an umbrella group of more than 20 other organizations, including the National Association for the Advancement of Colored People, the NEA, and the Southern Christian Leadership Conference, to establish the Youth Franchise Coalition in 1969. They advocated for 18-year-old voting rights by state legislation and by a national minimum age mandated by a constitutional amendment. In April, the NAACP held a nonpartisan and color-blind mobilization conference that drew over 2,000 delegates from 33 states. Appearances and behavior mattered to many activists who feared alienating public support due to radical student images.

Demonstration for reduction in voting age, Seattle, 1969 (MOHAI, Seattle Post-Intelligencer Collection, 1986.5.50631.1).

To national politicians, the vote continued to be seen as a means to quell unrest. In 1969, both a presidential commission established to investigate violence in society and an investigation by a group of House Republicans into campus unrest recommended a lowered voting age. In fact, a report of the NEA's Project 18 also cited that the far left opposed a lowered voting age that might cause young people to abandon radical causes.

In addition to curing societal ills, the path to the 18-year-old ballot could represent the logical next step in the expansion of voting rights that the '60s witnessed. The Vietnam War also broadened the conscription link given the particularly onerous burden borne by young people drafted into an unwanted conflict, as well as the increased participation of women in the military.

If the country could put a man on the moon by the end of the decade, perhaps putting a ballot to 18-year-olds no longer seemed such an out of space idea.

ONE SMALL STEP, ONE GIANT LEAP

1970s

AMERICA TURNED THE PAGE ON A NEW DECADE BUT ITS PROBLEMS SPILLED INTO HISTORY'S NEXT CHAPTER.

NEITHER VIETNAM NOR STUDENT ACTIVISM WAS GOING AWAY.

The public remained wary of student activism. Students remained wary of adults. Weary protestors found new vigor following the U.S. invasion of Cambodia at the end of April and the Kent State and Jackson State shootings in May.

Instead of rocketing higher, support for a lowered voting age fell from 66% in September 1968 to 58% in April 1970. Proposals in multiple states failed. On the state level, factors included citing threat to status quo, fear of student radicalism, confusion with other age-related issues such as drinking age and jury service, and an inadequately funded campaign.

On Capitol Hill, it did not appear any legislative action would break through the stalwart opposition posed by Rep. Celler's House Committee and concern over federal intrusion into state affairs despite growing bipartisan support. That apparent stalemate didn't stop the Subcommittee on Constitutional Amendments of the Senate Judiciary Committee holding hearings beginning in February (on the same day a law enfranchising 18-year-olds in Britain went into effect) regarding now Sen. Randolph's proposed constitutional amendment to lower the voting age to 18. Familiar arguments on both sides resurfaced.

What has so far been the missing ingredient in our efforts to lower the voting age is missing no longer. We now have it, it seems to me, a working alliance between young and old, Democrat and Republican, scholar and businessman, citizens from all across the country who are determined to press forward on every front...

... In addition to commemorating the 100th anniversary of Negro suffrage and the 50th anniversary of women's suffrage, I hope that we can mark 1970 as the birth of truly universal suffrage in America—by lowering the voting age and thus completing the long and historic democratic journey this nation began in 1789.

—SEN. BIRCH BAYH (D-IN)

We do not contend that all 18-to 21-year-old young people are models of perfection, but certainly there is no other group, no other age group, that is a model of perfection either. We believe, as I said, that this generation is probably the most knowledgeable generation and the most interested in government than any generation we have had.

They are frustrated. There is no question they are frustrated from the denial of this right to vote.

—NEA OFFICIAL JOHN M. LUMLEY

The Nixon Administration favored a constitutional amendment to lower the age for federal elections only. In its opinion, each state should determine its age requirement.

> I am not urging an across-the-board provision as in the existing 15th and 19th amendments because in my judgment age—unlike race and sex—may be a legitimate qualification on the right to vote.
>
> —Deputy Attorney General Richard G. Kleindienst

> [W]hat is the 'discrimination' which Congress would here seek to eliminate? Unless voting is to be done from the crib, the minimum age line must be drawn somewhere; can it really be said that to deny 20-, 19-, and 18-year-olds is 'discrimination,' while to deny the vote to 17-year-olds is sound legislative judgment?
>
> —Assistant Attorney General William H. Rehnquist

One nineteen-year-old researcher with the Youth Franchise Coalition called out "legislative procrastination" and noted the political dynamics.

> Legislators as a whole are difficult to motivate unless they see some benefit to themselves. More so, the unwillingness to act on this issue reflects fear on the part of the majority of legislators that an extension of the franchise will pose a threat to the security of their office ... I certainly hope, and somewhat believe, that we are presently here so that young citizens, who

> happen to be between the ages of 18 and 20, can best enjoy
> the democratic processes this country has made so much of
> her heritage.
>
> —ALAN M. DiSCULLO, YOUTH FRANCHISE COALITION

Not everyone was procrastinating. One young assistant to Sen. Edward M. Kennedy (D-MA) was burning the midnight oil reading up on the Constitution and recent Supreme Court decisions. Legislative aide Carey Parker sought to understand the relationship between the Constitution and voting rights laws.

BURNING THE MIDNIGHT OIL

While the voting age issue had remained stalled in state legislatures and Congressional bureaucracy, the federal government addressed equal rights concerns of disaffected groups through anti-discrimination policies. In particular, voting rights had become a chief focus of concern of Congress and the Supreme Court since the mid-60s. Under Chief Justice Earl Warren, who had retired in mid-1969, the Supreme Court had relied on the Equal Protection Clause of the Fourteenth Amendment to rule in several cases in favor of federal intervention into discriminatory state voting practices.

> All persons born or naturalized in the United States, and subject to the jurisdiction thereof, are citizens of the United States and of the State wherein they reside. No State shall make or enforce any law which shall abridge the privileges or immunities of citizens of the United States; nor shall any State deprive any person of life, liberty, or property, without due process of law; nor deny to any person within its jurisdiction **the equal protection of the laws.**
>
> —U.S. CONSTITUTION,
> Amendment XIV, Section 1 (emphasis added)

At a time of heightened federal protection of minority voting rights, national politicians and lowered voting age activists began to view 18-21-year-olds as a class that similarly experienced discrimination at the polls.

Remember that law review article written in 1966 by Harvard Law Prof. Archibald Cox? Well, Parker stumbled across it.

> **Eureka, Cox has given us the argument we need.**
>
> —CAREY PARKER

"EUREKA!"

He sent a memo to his boss describing Prof. Cox's view that Congress could reduce the voting age to 18 by statute instead of by a constitutional amendment. Sen. Kennedy soon circulated the memo to other members of the Senate Judiciary Committee.

TWO GREAT TASTES

SOMETIMES A NEW STRATEGY CAN BREAK THROUGH A STICKY STALEMATE.

TAKE CHOCOLATE AND PEANUT BUTTER, FOR EXAMPLE.

MOST FOLKS AGREE THAT THIS COMBINATION IS SUBLIME. BUT IT WASN'T ALWAYS SO ASSUMED.

IN 1970, SEVEN YEARS AFTER THE HERSHEY COMPANY BOUGHT H.B. REESE CANDY COMPANY, THE MANUFACTURER THAT HAD BEEN MAKING PEANUT BUTTER CUPS SINCE 1928, A NEW NATIONAL ADVERTISING PITCH COMMENCED. THE CAMPAIGN AIMED TO CONVINCE THE PUBLIC THAT THE HUMBLE PEANUT BUTTER CUP COMBINED "TWO GREAT TASTES THAT TASTE GREAT TOGETHER."

IT WORKED. THE SUCCESSFUL MARKETING JOLTED SALES BY EFFECTIVELY REBRANDING THE SWEET AND SALTY CANDY AND MAKING IT SEEM NEW AND EXCITING.

Likewise *(well, sort of)*, civil rights and the voting age were two great causes that worked great together. Since 1967, civil rights leaders had formed closer ties with anti-war activists. Embracing the 18-year-old vote was a natural evolution.

And timing can be everything. To beat the clock on certain sections of the landmark Voting Rights Act due to expire on August 6, 1970, the Senate had begun reaching bipartisan support on a proposal by Senate Minority Leader Hugh Scott (R-PA) and Sen. Philip Hart (D-MI) to reauthorize the act with only limited modifications.

BEAT THE CLOCK: VOTING RIGHTS EDITION

Sen. Kennedy had one more modification to suggest. Based on Parker's research, he proposed adding a rider to the Voting Rights Act that would authorize 18-year-old voting. The language for the rider was modeled on a provision of the Voting Rights Act that effectively banned a New York English literacy test requirement for prospective voters which discriminated against the local Puerto Rican community and had passed Supreme Court muster in the 1966 decision *Katzenbach v. Morgan*. In that case, the Court found the discrimination as an unconstitutional violation of the Fourteenth Amendment's Equal Protection Clause and pointed to Section 5 of the amendment as authority for Congress to enforce the Equal Protection clause by appropriate legislation.

> The Congress shall have the power to enforce, by appropriate legislation, the provisions of this article.
>
> —U.S. CONSTITUTION, AMEND. XIV, § 5

According to this logic, Sen. Kennedy asserted denial of the vote to 18-21-year-olds as representing discrimination that violated the Equal Protection Clause and which thereby Congress had a constitutional right to remedy.

> Just as Congress has the power to find an English literacy test discriminates against Spanish-speaking Americans, so Congress has the power to recognize the increased education and maturity of our youth, and to find discrimination in the fact that young Americans who fight, work, marry, and pay taxes like other citizens are denied the right to vote, the most basic right of all.
>
> —SEN. EDWARD M. KENNEDY (D-MA)

Despite bipartisan interest, political realities interfered with his plan. Some House members fretted about how an influx of young voters might impact their base. The behind the scenes opposition of these individuals signaled that a stand-alone bill for 18-year-old voting would have failed in the House. Civil rights leaders worried about undermining their chances of securing an extension of the Voting Rights Act. Sen. Kennedy heeded the concerns and the Voting Rights Act of 1970 did not include the voting age amendment when it passed the Senate Judiciary Committee.

And then a GROOVY thing happened.

Sen. Kennedy's proposal was carjacked. On a winter night while Sen. Kennedy was abroad, Sen. Majority Leader Mike Mansfield (D-MT) gave Sen. Warren Magnuson (D-WA) a ride home.

VOTING AGE AMENDMENT CARJACKED

Their car ride conversation drove the voting age amendment into uncharted territory. They thought they could successively hitch the issue to the Voting Rights Act extension soon to be considered by the full House. At Sen. Magnuson's suggestion, Sen. Mansfield agreed to attach the lowered voting age amendment to the Scott-Hart Bill when it came to a vote on the floor.

On March 4, Sen. Mansfield did just that by introducing a provision establishing 18 as the minimum voting age in all federal, state, and local elections. Sen. Kennedy, who knew nothing of this maneuvering that occurred while he was away, joined as a co-sponsor the next day.

GOOD FOR 18–21–YEAR–OLDS.
GOOD FOR CONGRESSIONAL CARPOOLING.
NOT SO GOOD FOR REP. CELLER.

Since his "stinky cheese" spiel sixteen years earlier, Rep. Celler's opposition to 18-year-old voting had only festered and he used his chairmanship of the House Judiciary Committee to thwart all attempts to lower the age. Yet, though he abhorred a lowered voting age, he revered the Voting Rights Act. Rep. Celler found himself backed into a corner.

Still, the question of Congressional authority to legislate a lowered voting age cast a shadow over the amendment. No longer did the very concept of 18-year-old voting stir much controversy in the Senate when deliberations resumed on March 9 in the Senate Subcommittee on Constitutional Amendments. Instead, debate centered more on whether to lower the voting age by statute or by amendment.

> The voting age should be lowered and lowered at once across the entire Nation.
>
> To my mind, the change can validly be achieved through a constitutional amendment or statute. For once a person reaches the conclusion, as I have, that there is no reasonable justification for denying the right to vote to 18-year-olds, then it is quite clear that Congress can act to protect and enhance that right.
>
> —SEN. BARRY GOLDWATER (R-AZ)

> The disenfranchisement of approximately 10 million young Americans deserves, warrants and demands the attention of the NAACP. We can find no moral, legal, or political reason to justify keeping these young people on the outside of the decisionmaking arena of this country.
>
> —JAMES BROWN, JR., NAACP NATIONAL YOUTH DIRECTOR

> As long as they are disenfranchised they are placed in an anomalous position of weakness where they ought to have strength, they are outside the system where they ought to be inside the system . . .
>
> . . . I think it is exceedingly important that it be done at once. . .
>
> . . . I think they will be very discouraged if after this conspicuous display of interest and bipartisan sponsorship nothing happens again.
>
> —DR. MARGARET MEAD, PROFESSOR OF
> ANTHROPOLOGY, COLUMBIA UNIVERSITY

Long-time rivals Harvard and Yale squabbled unofficially through a scrimmage of their legal minds. A cadre of Yale Law School professors took aim at the arguments advanced by Prof. Cox and echoed by his colleague, Prof. Paul Freund. The two sides faced off on the editorial pages of the *New York Times* and in congressional testimony.

> I strongly endorse the proposal to reduce the voting age to 18 in elections, both Federal and State . . .
>
> . . . I submit that it must be plain that Congress has no plenary sort of authority over voting qualifications . . .
>
> . . . I am doubtful about Katzenbach v. Morgan as a basis for proceeding here by statute, and as to why, even if I am wrong in my doubts I would be skeptical about proceeding by statute as opposed to a constitutional amendment.
>
> —LOUIS POLLAK, DEAN OF YALE LAW SCHOOL

On the Senate floor, even allies bickered.

None other than Sen. Randolph sought to continue down the potentially more arduous path of pursuing a constitutional amendment. Sen. Mansfield became irritated with Sen. Randolph's repeated assurances that an amendment would pass quickly.

> **Mr. President, there is no question that the Senate could approve the Constitutional amendment by the two-thirds plurality necessary.**
>
> **—SEN. JENNINGS RANDOLPH (D-WV)**

> **The distinguished Senator from West Virginia himself has been introducing resolutions [for a constitutional amendment] since 1942, and where are they? Still in committee. Where are they when Congress adjourns? Dead.**
>
> **This is a chance to put sentiment to the test, and if you believe in giving the vote to the 18-year-olds, this is the time and the way to do it. It is not only appropriate but our last clear chance in this Congress.**
>
> **—SEN. MIKE MANSFIELD (D-MT)**

On March 13, by a 64 to 12 vote, the Senate passed the extension of the Voting Rights Act that included the Kennedy-Mansfield amendment to lower the voting age to 18 for all elections beginning in 1971.

The bill passed with one key amendment. It came from Sen. James Allen (D-AL) who had tried to derail the bill's passage several times by introducing handwritten amendments one at a time during the debate. That one of them actually passed surprised even him, as he recounted on the Senate floor three months later.

> So, far from handing out literary and verbal bouquets at this time to the House of Representatives on the passage of this statutory provision, I think that we should take stock of just what we have done and hope that we will have an early decision of the Supreme Court of the United States . . .
>
> One amendment that I offered was adopted on the Senate floor. It was accepted, to my surprise, by the Senate. It was offered almost in jest, because I had been one of a group of Senators who had supported certain legislation which had been emasculated by a similar provision. The legislation to which I refer was almost completely emasculated by putting in the phrase "except as required by the Constitution," . . .
>
> So it may well be that this phrase, put into the law somewhat in jest, will be a significant feature when the measure is before the Supreme Court for decision.
>
> —SEN. JAMES ALLEN (D-AL)

Passing the Voting Rights Act as amended and approved by the Senate was no laughing matter to Rep. Celler. Placing a priority on securing the civil rights legislation over his minimum voting age objections, Rep. Celler now caved and dug himself out of his quagmire by acquiescing to the lowered voting age provision.

Not only that, in order to avoid any possibility that the House might make further changes that would then result in the bill going to a conference committee, he chose to bypass the usual legislative process and instead engineered a means where the Senate bill would be voted on the House floor after only a one hour debate.

On June 17, 1970, the full House finally debated the voting age issue for the first time. Rep. Celler immediately laid out the situation. He warned about allowing the Voting Rights Act to expire and the dangers of sending the bill back to the Senate where he feared a filibuster.

I want to point out to you my good friends that a vote against [the resolution] is tantamount to a vote against the extension of the Voting Rights Act...

... If this bill goes back to the other body, then this bill is as dead as that flightless bird called the dodo...

... The statutory voting age reduction provision will meet an early court challenge this year. It will receive a full and complete review by the Supreme Court before the end of the year and a final judicial determination will occur before the 1971 elections...

... Unlike many Members, I do hold doubts as to the wisdom of extending the franchise to persons 18 to 21...

I also hold reservations about the constitutional authority of Congress to statutorily amend voting age requirements in State and local, as well as Federal, elections. Nor do I find decisions of the Supreme Court that hold or intimate that the

> Congress, by legislative fiat, may declare nationwide voting age requirements...
>
> Despite these reservations and concerns, to which, as you know, I have given vent recently, I am now, today, firmly and finally of the opinion that we must brook no obstacle to the immediate extension of the Voting Rights Act of 1965. That extension is of such paramount national importance that it must be effectuated as promptly as possible and at a minimum of risk.
>
> —REP. EMANUEL CELLER (D-NY)

Debate on the House floor revisited policy and constitutional concerns and politicians also chafed at the constraints imposed on their deliberations.

AH...THE BEAUTY AND ELOQUENCE OF DEMOCRACY IN ACTION...

> Mr. Speaker, the Senate amendment lowering the voting age to 18 shares a common evil with the 1965 Voting Rights Act, to which it is attached; both trample on the rights of the States.
>
> —REP. GEORGE ANDREWS (D-AL)

> How ridiculous can we become in our effort to evade proper constitutional processes. Well, it has been said before: there is no end to the folly of man.
>
> Let us be done with this charade; with this flimsily disguised seizure of power.
>
> —REP. LAWRENCE FOUNTAIN (D-NC)

This Congress cannot claim to be upholding and enforcing the 14th Amendment, which provides for the equal protection of the law, when it denies the right to vote to these individuals who are so informed about the issues of our society and who have so great a stake in their content.

—REP. BERTRAM PODELL (D-NY)

There are two groups in our Nation which are excluded from the elective process in significant numbers—black citizens and those young people under 21. This legislative package is aimed at bringing to significant numbers in both groups the right of suffrage.

—REP. HOWARD ROBISON (R-NY)

If we adopt this rule the House agrees that it is the second-class body of the Congress. I cannot understand why so many seem so intent to eliminate ourselves as a legislative body.

—REP. WILLIAM RANDALL (D- MO)

This proposition is coming to the floor of the House under the most indefensible combination of legislation and parliamentary procedure I have ever seen.

—REP. GERALD FORD (R-MI)

> We might just as well quit and ask the other body what they think we ought to do over here; and permit them to write the legislation in the first place.
>
> —REP. WILLIAM COLMER (D-MS)

The House didn't quit. They voted. One hour later, the resolution passed by a greater than 2:1 margin. Packed with young people, the House gallery burst into applause.

On June 22, 1970, despite voicing reservations about the law's constitutionality and continuing to advocate for a constitutional amendment, Pres. Nixon signed into law the amended Voting Rights Act that lowered the voting age in all federal, state, and local elections to 18.

> The time has also come to give 18-year-olds the vote, as I have long urged. The way to do this is by amending the Constitution. Because of the likelihood that the 18-year-old vote provisions of this law will not survive its court test, the constitutional amendment pending before the Congress should go forward to the states for ratification now.
>
> —PRESIDENT RICHARD M. NIXON

And just like that, nearly twenty-eight years after the first legislation was proposed, the legislative and executive branches of the federal government decided 18-year-olds should vote.

PEN PSYCHOLOGY 101

PRESIDENTS TYPICALLY HOST A CEREMONY WHEN SIGNING A HISTORIC BILL INTO LAW AND AFTERWARDS DISTRIBUTING SOUVENIR PENS TO GUESTS.

FOR EXAMPLE, PRES. JOHNSON BESTOWED 75 PENS AS MEMENTOS TO HIS AUDIENCE WHEN HE AUTHORIZED THE 1964 CIVIL RIGHTS ACT.

PERHAPS PRES. NIXON LET ARMCHAIR PSYCHOLOGISTS KNOW HIS TRUE FEELINGS ABOUT THE VOTING AGE LEGISLATION BY SIGNING IT IN HIS HIDEAWAY OFFICE SHORTLY AFTER LUNCH.

HE USED HIS OWN SILVER FOUNTAIN PEN AND HAD ONLY ONE AIDE IN ATTENDANCE.

NOTE:

WHEN PRES. NIXON RESIGNED IN 1974, HE SIGNED HIS RESIGNATION LETTER WITH A FELT TIP PEN IN PRIVATE AFTER DINING ON A BREAKFAST OF CORNED BEEF HASH AND POACHED EGGS.

NO SOUVENIR PENS NEEDED.

II. COULD THEY?

BUT COULD 18-YEAR-OLD AMERICANS VOTE? REALLY?

Technically, yes. It was now the written law of the land that 18-year olds could vote in federal and state elections. But, as promised, that was about to be challenged. It would now be up to the federal judiciary to weigh in on the issue.

Pres. Nixon had signed into law the provisions of the Voting Rights Act of 1970 that included lowered the voting age but he also signed off on testing its constitutionality.

> Despite my misgivings about the constitutionality of this one provision, I have signed the bill. I have directed the Attorney General to cooperate fully in expediting a swift court test of the constitutionality of the 18-year-old provision.
>
> —PRESIDENT RICHARD M. NIXON

The ink was barely dry on his signature when legal challenges began. Five New Yorkers immediately challenged the law. Meanwhile, Attorney Gen. John N. Mitchell reportedly had no intention of initiating a legal test. His recalcitrance led some to wonder whether the Nixon Administration now thought young people might tilt more conservative than liberal.

In mid-July, the Attorney Gen. directed all states to produce written assurances of compliance with the new law by August 3. Only twenty states produced the requested written assurances of compliance with the eighteen-year-old voting provision by the deadline. North Carolina said no way, they were not going to abide by either the younger voting provision or the literacy test ban. Oregon and other states said that without a federal court ruling they could not disregard their own state constitutions that set twenty-one as the minimum voting age.

The judicial branch now took its turn at the dance. Oregon and Texas had filed suit on August 3 to contest the law's constitutionality. The U.S. Justice Department filed suit against Idaho and Arizona two weeks later for non-compliance with the voting age provisions. These legal challenges came to a head with *Oregon v. Mitchell*, a Supreme Court case argued on Oct. 19, 1970 and decided on Dec. 21, 1970.

(In the interim, fifteen states held referenda on the voting age. Maine and Nebraska lowered the age to twenty, Montana and Massachusetts dropped theirs to nineteen, and Alaska lowered its age to eighteen. Voters in Colorado, Connecticut, Florida, Hawaii, Michigan, Minnesota, New Jersey, South Dakota, Washington, and Wyoming rejected lowered voting age proposals in their states.)

A TIPPING POINT?

In a 5-4 decision, the Court ruled that Congress had the authority under the First and Fourteenth Amendments to lower the voting age by statute for federal elections only. That meant the Court upheld the statute's provisions allowing 18-year-old voting in federal elections but struck down the lowered age for state and local elections.

Justice Hugo Black wrote the majority opinion—which, given Supreme Court math, turned out to be a majority of one. The brethren squabbled amongst themselves. Four justices concurred and dissented in part.

Justice Black cited various constitutional bases to find that Congress could make laws regarding federal elections. However, he did not believe that Congress possessed authority under the Fourteenth Amendment to address state voter qualifications.

> **Since Congress has attempted to invade an area preserved to the States by the Constitution without a foundation for enforcing the Civil War Amendments' ban on racial discrimination, I would hold that Congress has exceeded its powers in attempting to lower the voting age in state and local elections. On the other hand, where Congress legislates in a domain not exclusively reserved by the Constitution to the States, its enforcement power need not be tied so closely to the goal of eliminating discrimination on account of race.**
>
> **—JUSTICE HUGO BLACK**

Justices William J. Brennan Jr., William O. Douglas, Thurgood Marshall, and Byron White maintained that the voting age provision was constitutional for both federal and state elections.

Justice Douglas viewed the right to vote as a fundamental civil right protected by the Fourteenth Amendment. He believed Congress had the power to determine the age of maturity that would entitle one to vote.

> **It is a reasoned judgment that those who have such a large "stake" in modern elections as 18-year-olds whether, in times of war or peace, should have political equality. ...the Equal Protection Clause does service to protect the right to vote in federal as well as in state elections.**
>
> **—JUSTICE WILLIAM O. DOUGLAS**

Justice Brennan issued a separate opinion, joined by Justices White and Marshall, that argued Congress acted legitimately under its power to enforce the Fourteenth Amendment.

> **In sum, Congress had ample evidence upon which it could have based the conclusion that exclusion of citizens 18 to 21 years of age from the franchise is wholly unnecessary to promote any legitimate interest the States may have in assuring intelligent and responsible voting. If discrimination is unnecessary to promote any legitimate state interest, it is plainly unconstitutional under the Equal Protection Clause, and Congress has ample power to forbid it under Section 5 of the Fourteenth Amendment.**
>
> **—JUSTICE WILLIAM J. BRENNAN JR.**

The other four justices thought the voting age provision was unconstitutional in either federal or state elections.

Justice John M. Harlan penned a lengthy opinion that examined the legislative history of the Fourteenth Amendment and disagreed with just about everything that Justices Douglas and Brennan had written. For him, Congress could not intervene in state voting requirements without evidence of unconstitutional discrimination.

> the suggestion that members of the age group between 18 and 21 are threatened with unconstitutional discrimination, or that any hypothetical discrimination is likely to be affected by lowering the voting age, is little short of fanciful.
>
> —JUSTICE JOHN M. HARLAN

Justice Potter Stewart, joined by Chief Justice Warren E. Burger and Justice Harry Blackmun, emphasized that states had the constitutional power to set voting qualifications and that Congress could not intervene absent a compelling interest. Age qualifications, though interesting in and of themselves, did not represent a constitutionally compelling interest.

> A casual reader could easily get the impression that what we are being asked in these cases is whether or not we think allowing people 18 years old to vote is a good idea. Nothing could be wider of the mark. My Brothers to the contrary, there is no question here as to the judgment of Congress; there are questions only of Congress' constitutional power.
>
> —JUSTICE POTTER STEWART

If the Supreme Court's arithmetic seemed complex, their decision caused infinitesimal more headaches for the forty-seven states that had minimum voting ages over 18. It would mean that these states would need to have a dual voting system, with one age limit for federal elections and another for state elections.

One solution might be for states to amend their constitutions to allow for 18-year old voting, but there might not be enough time to do so before the 1972 presidential elections. Another position could be to take the opposite policy stance and repeal the voting age amendment to the Voting Rights Act, but this idea lacked significant support. The remaining solution—one that had already been kicking around the halls of Congress and endorsed by Pres. Nixon—would be to pass a constitutional amendment that settled the issue.

Congress sprang into action with two familiar faces taking charge. On March 10, the Senate passed Sen. Randolph's joint resolution that called for a constitutional amendment to lower the voting age to 18 in federal and state elections. Noting that the voting age movement had gained an irreversible momentum, Rep. Celler co-sponsored an identical proposal in the House.

> [A]ny effort to stop the wave for the 18-year-old vote would be as useless as a telescope to a blind man.
>
> —REP. EMANUEL CELLER (D-NY)

18-YEAR-OLD VOTING AGE APPEARS IN SIGHT

Once again, objections regarding states' rights surfaced from some southern Democrats and conservative Republicans. This time, on March 23, the House voted overwhelmingly to pass the joint resolution calling for a proposed constitutional amendment.

(Rep. Celler was feeling particularly loquacious that day. Two months shy of his 83rd birthday, he remarked, "By offering this amendment, perhaps I can again wear the robes of youth." If ratified, he noted that his sponsorship would make the amendment "the fourth coonskin for my door.")

S. J. Res. 7

Ninety-second Congress of the United States of America

AT THE FIRST SESSION

Begun and held at the City of Washington on Thursday, the twenty-first day of January, one thousand nine hundred and seventy-one

Joint Resolution

Proposing an amendment to the Constitution of the United States extending the right to vote to citizens eighteen years of age or older.

Resolved by the Senate and House of Representatives of the United States of America in Congress assembled (two-thirds of each House concurring therein), That the following article is proposed as an amendment to the Constitution of the United States, which shall be valid to all intents and purposes as part of the Constitution when ratified by the legislatures of three-fourths of the several States within seven years from the date of its submission by the Congress:

"ARTICLE —

"SECTION 1. The right of citizens of the United States, who are eighteen years of age or older, to vote shall not be denied or abridged by the United States or by any State on account of age.

"SEC. 2. The Congress shall have power to enforce this article by appropriate legislation."

Carl Albert
Speaker of the House of Representatives.

Allen J. Ellender
Vice President of the United States and
President of the Senate pro tempore.

Joint Resolution Proposing 26th Amendment to the U.S. Constitution; Passed by Congress March 23, 1971. (National Archives).

Now, on to the states.

The Congress, whenever two thirds of both houses shall deem it necessary, shall propose amendments to this Constitution, or, on the application of the legislatures of two thirds of the several states, shall call a convention for proposing amendments, which, in either case, shall be valid to all intents and purposes, as part of this Constitution, when ratified by the legislatures of three fourths of the several states, or by conventions in three fourths thereof, as the one or the other mode of ratification may be proposed by the Congress; provided that no amendment which may be made prior to the year one thousand eight hundred and eight shall in any manner affect the first and fourth clauses in the ninth section of the first article; and that no state, without its consent, shall be deprived of its equal suffrage in the Senate.

—U.S. CONSTITUTION, ARTICLE V

Nothing says sibling rivalry like a race to ratification. Many states may want to be first but no one wants to be 39th. Within an hour after the House vote, Minnesota and Delaware vied with each other to first ratify the amendment while Connecticut, Washington, and Tennessee also approved it that day. Despite some debates regarding federal intrusion into state affairs and whether their own constituents had rejected a lowered age in past referendums, states jumped onboard quickly in a political environment that generally supported the amendment. The Youth Franchise Coalition and Common Cause helped lead lobbying efforts. In the sprint to be 38th, the magic number needed to amend the Constitution, just after Alabama and North Carolina ratified the amendment earlier that day, Ohio in an "atmosphere of near-panic" to beat out Oklahoma crossed the line on the night of June 30, 1971.

At least that's what was reported and what Pres. Nixon also thought. That night, he issued a statement congratulating the nation's "young citizens" on gaining the vote.

> Some 11 million young men and women who have participated in the life of our nation through their work, their studies, and their sacrifices for its defense, are now to be fully included in the electoral process of our country...
>
> The ratification of this amendment has been accomplished in the shortest time of any amendment in American history. This fact affirms our nation's confidence in its youth and its trust in their responsibility. It also reinforces our young people's dedication to a system of government whose constitution permits ordered change.
>
> I urge them to honor this right—by registering and voting in each election.
>
> —PRESIDENT RICHARD M. NIXON

Just like the first state to ratify may be disputed, so, too, was the last state and date. Based on a required review by the General Services Administration of official state documents, both the National Archives and the Library of Congress recognize North Carolina as the 38th state to ratify the 26th Amendment on July 1, 1971, right after Ohio and ahead of Oklahoma.

On July 5, 1971, amid great fanfare in the East Room with a mid-afternoon performance by 500 members of a national youth honors choral group, General Services Admin. Robert Kunzig officially certified the Twenty-Sixth Amendment as valid.

Although presidents have no mandated role in the certification of an amendment, Pres. Nixon couldn't help himself. Leaning over the same desk Thomas Jefferson had used at the Continental Congress, he signed as a witness. The other witnesses were chosen by the choral group's director who had been told earlier by Chief of Staff H.R. Haldeman that the president stipulated that each be 18, and include one African American, one Caucasian, one male, one female, and from the South, Midwest, and California.

President Nixon signs 26ᵗʰ Amendment in certification ceremony. (WHPO-6749-010A) (courtesy The Richard Nixon Presidential Library and Museum).

THIS TIME, HE BROUGHT SOME EXTRA PENS. The three selected young singers (Paul S. Larimer, Joseph W. Loyd, Jr., and Julianne Jones, pictured above) signed as official witnesses. They kept the pens.

> **Every time I go and vote, I think, 'This is really cool that I had a little bit to do with, hopefully, young people taking an interest in their country.'**
>
> —JULIANNE [JONES] SHAPARD, REMINISCING IN 2018 ABOUT HER ROLE

And just like that (again), 18-year-olds really could vote.

STILL MORE ABOUT PENS
AND NOW SOMETHING ABOUT PUNCH, TOO

ALL THE CHOIR MEMBERS ALSO RECEIVED SOUVENIR PENS, BUT ONLY AFTER TRICKY DICK FIRST TEASED THEM BY SAYING, "I WISH WE HAD 500 MORE PENS, BUT THAT IS ABOVE OUR BUDGET."

HIS REMARKS INCLUDED COMMENTARY ON THE REFRESHMENTS, NOTING THAT "THE PUNCH IS VERY GOOD, AND IT IS MADE FROM FLORIDA AND CALIFORNIA PRODUCTS. BUT AS FAR AS THE HOME COOKING IS CONCERNED, I FOUND THAT THE COOKIES WERE MADE BY A SWISS CHEF, BUT THEY ALSO WILL BE VERY GOOD."

HUH? THIS FROM THE GUY WHO OFTEN ATE COTTAGE CHEESE WITH KETCHUP??

HE CONCLUDED HIS ADDRESS BY STATING, "BY THE WAY, IN CHECKING AT THE WAREHOUSE, WE FIND WE DO HAVE ENOUGH PENS FOR ALL 500 OF YOU."

PHEW.

Nixon, Richard M. *Richard M. Nixon's Notes for 26th Amendment Ceremony, July 5, 1971.* (National Archives, Identifier 1634228).

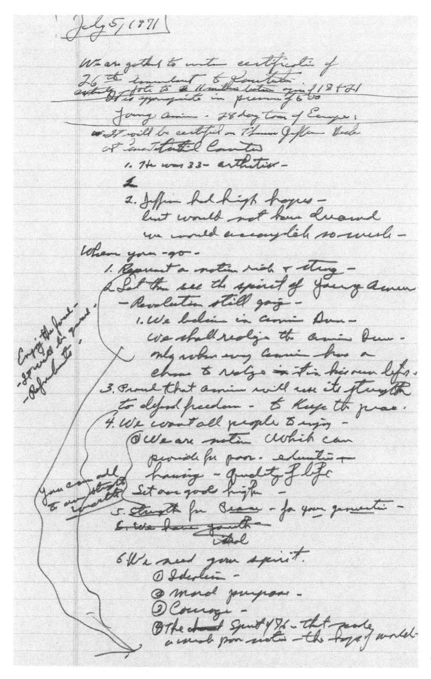

Nixon, Richard M. *Richard M. Nixon's Notes for 26th Amendment Ceremony, July 5, 1971.*
(National Archives, Identifier 1634228)

ADMINISTRATOR OF GENERAL SERVICES

UNITED STATES OF AMERICA

TO ALL TO WHOM THESE PRESENTS SHALL COME,

GREETING:

KNOW YE, That the Congress of the United States, at the first session, Ninety-second Congress begun at the City of Washington on Thursday, the twenty-first day of January, in the year one thousand nine hundred and seventy-one, passed a Joint Resolution in the words and figures as follows: to wit--

JOINT RESOLUTION

Proposing an amendment to the Constitution of the United States extending the right to vote to citizens eighteen years of age or older.

Resolved by the Senate and House of Representatives of the United States of America in Congress assembled (two-thirds of each House concurring therein), That the following article is proposed as an amendment to the Constitution of the United States, which shall be valid to all intents and purposes as part of the Constitution when ratified by the legislatures of three-fourths of the several States within seven years from the date of its submission by the Congress:

"ARTICLE —

"Section 1. The right of citizens of the United States, who are eighteen years of age or older, to vote shall not be denied or abridged by the United States or by any State on account of age.
"Sec. 2. The Congress shall have power to enforce this article by appropriate legislation."

And, further, that it appears from official documents on file in the General Services Administration that the Amendment to the Constitution of the United States proposed as aforesaid has been ratified by the Legislatures of the States of Alabama, Alaska, Arizona, Arkansas, California, Colorado,

Twenty-Sixth Amendment. U.S. National Archives.

Connecticut, Delaware, Hawaii, Idaho, Illinois, Indiana, Iowa, Kansas, Louisiana, Maine, Maryland, Massachusetts, Michigan, Minnesota, Missouri, Montana, Nebraska, New Hampshire, New Jersey, New York, North Carolina, Ohio, Oklahoma, Oregon, Pennsylvania, Rhode Island, South Carolina, Tennessee, Texas, Vermont, Washington, West Virginia, and Wisconsin.

And, further, that the States whose Legislatures have so ratified the said proposed Amendment constitute the requisite three-fourths of the whole number of States in the United States.

NOW, Therefore, be it known that I, Robert L. Kunzig, Administrator of General Services, by virtue and in pursuance of Section 106b, Title 1 of the United States Code, do hereby certify that the Amendment aforesaid has become valid, to all intents and purposes, as a part of the Constitution of the United States.

IN TESTIMONY WHEREOF,

I have hereunto set my hand and caused the seal of the General Services Administration to be affixed.

DONE at the City of Washington this 5th day of July in the year of our Lord one thousand nine hundred and seventy-one.

ROBERT L. KUNZIG

The foregoing was signed in our presence on this 5th day of July, 1971.

Paul I. Larimer

Joseph H. Laud Jr.

Julianne Jones

[Questions for Constitutional sleuths: Was Julianne the first female to sign a Constitutional amendment? Was Joseph the first African American to do so?]

III. WOULD THEY?

FROM THERE TO HERE

On Election Day 1972, long-haired youth crowded the polling stations and changed the political equation for ever more.

Well, not exactly.

About half of the nation's 11 million newly eligible voters between 18-20-years-old actually turned out to vote, below expectations.

But at least they turned up/but even so, they never showed up in such numbers again. NEVER.

(Not yet, anyway. That's where YOU come in.)

So what explains this?

Reasons cited:

Apathy.
Ignorance.
Slacktivism.

But these criticisms are not entirely accurate nor are young people wholly to blame. Youth have shown themselves to be politically active and engaged—those were some of the reasons cited for extending them the vote in the first place.

Other reasons suggest that higher youth turnout is often tied to the candidacy of a charismatic personality leader, a unifying issue, and targeted campaign outreach. Factors contributing to lower turnout include a lack of civics education, issues related to registration difficulties given young voters' transiency, few voting places near college campuses, as well as plain unabashed obstruction from those fearing their voting preferences.

Since young people won the vote, presidential candidates have often paid little attention to them given their lack of relative financial resources to fund campaigns, transiency, presumed apathy, and unreliability in actually turning up at the ballot box. Those who recognized their potential strength often benefitted.

Here's a brief overview of what REALLY HAPPENED with the youth vote over the years.

(For each general presidential election described below, the Democratic and Republican nominees are specified, with the victor's name specified first.)

1972 Richard M. Nixon v. George McGovern
Voter Turnout
18-24: 49.6%
total: 63.0%

Although most directly affected by the Vietnam War and the draft, young voters also comprised the lowest turnout of all age groups (as they would in every presidential contest since then). And they didn't vote the way conventional wisdom thought, either. Relatively few college students took an active role in campaigning, many of whom identified themselves as Independents. Instead of solidly backing George McGovern who opposed the Vietnam War and supported liberal positions, nearly half of young first-time voters between 18-24 opted for Richard Nixon and contributed to his landslide victory.

Nixon hadn't just gotten lucky. The "good karma" that young folks felt toward him wasn't just organic, but encouraged. Despite McGovern's strong appeal to young voters in the primaries, the president's campaign recognized that not all young people went to college and they poured more resources into courting the working and unemployed youth vote than any other part of their campaign.

1976 Jimmy Carter v. Gerald Ford
Voter Turnout
18-24: 42.2%
total: 59.2%

Disillusioned by Watergate and uninspired by the primaries, both the general population and young voters stayed home in the 1976 presidential election when an enigmatic Washington outsider won the White House. A Census Bureau report attributed the overall lowest level of participation since 1948 on the apathy of new young voters, whose participation dropped more sharply than any other age group. Unnoticed by the Census data, the two major political parties had also decreased their attention to maintaining active youth affiliates and many schools were wary about the potential of political campaigning informing school activities.

1980 Ronald Reagan v. Jimmy Carter
Voter Turnout
18-24: 39.9%
total: 59.2%

Rampant inflation, unemployment, and the Iran hostage crisis soured the electorate on the Carter presidency and provided charismatic Ronald

Reagan a landslide victory in an election that also featured independent and former Republican primary candidate Rep. John B. Anderson. Although Reagan lagged behind Carter's share of the 18-21 year-old vote by 6%, he still drew a significant 41% share of that age group which saw its overall participation slightly decline while the older age groups stepped up their rate by over 3%.

1984 Ronald Reagan v. Walter Mondale
Voter Turnout
18-24: 40.8%
total   59.9%

"LADIES AND GENTLEMEN, ROCK 'N' ROLL."

A new player emerged in presidential politics in 1984 and its name was MTV. Presidential politics would never be the same.

Launched in 1981, the cable channel featured rock videos for its large young audience. Reagan campaign strategist Lee Atwater recognized that its popularity might help Republicans gain further traction with young voters. He sent Pres. Reagan a music video of John Cougar Mellencamp (no fan of Reagan himself). Whether Reagan watched it or not is unknown, but network announcers reported on Atwater's request and displayed a picture of Pres. Reagan with the caption "Does this man like MTV?"

Through commercials on rock music radio stations, television, and campus events, the Republican party devoted more resources than the Democrats to courting the youth vote. Although many young people did not agree with the Republican agenda on social issues, they found the Gipper and his pro-business and foreign policies likeable. Pres. Reagan's share of the 18-21 year-old vote climbed to 60% in the 1984 election. Young voters had shifted their party preference.

This shift did not go unnoticed. Intent on capturing this demographic, pollsters of both parties began scrutinizing music videos with as much intensity as their other statistics to discover the mindset of the potential youth vote. Some Democratic pollsters even considered the waning of punk rock as an indicator of renewed idealism.

1988 George H. W. Bush v. Michael Dukakis
Voter Turnout
18-24: 36.2%
total: 57.4%

The beat was not changing fast enough to stem the youth Republican tilt. By the 1988 election, 62% of voters under age 29 preferred George Bush.

MADONNA ROCKS THE VOTE

Even so, getting youth to actually go out and vote remained a problem for both parties. The overall population turnout dropped while the participation of younger voters fell to its lowest rate since gaining the vote. With only 10 million of its 25 million viewers registered to vote, MTV worked with Rock the Vote, a nonprofit founded in 1990 to fight music censorship and to engage youth politically, to promote registration. That year, the Material Girl turned Political as Madonna appeared in MTV's first ad to encourage midterm voting.

1992 Bill Clinton v. George H. W. Bush
Voter Turnout
18-24: 42.8%
total: 61.3%

Two years later, MTV no longer only showcased rock stars, it now featured presidential candidates looking to win over the audience. In an effort to help young people understand the candidates and issues, network reporters invited candidates to come on air and address their audience, and in particular, what it called the three E's of concern to young people: the economy, education, and the environment.

Bill Clinton stole the show. Appearing in front of a live forum of young questioners, he appeared to enjoy himself and provided one of the most remembered lines in campaign discourse when asked about his past marijuana use. When a questioner asked,"If you had it to do over again, would you inhale?", Clinton gamely replied, "Sure, if I could. I tried before."

Scrambling to catch up, both President Bush and independent candidate Ross Perot gave taped interviews. Neither played particularly well with the young set. Bush, who had previously dismissed MTV as a "teenybopper" network, appeared defensive on various subjects, including his veto of the motor-voter bill that would have allowed for voter registration at the time of getting a license. Still, at least viewers weren't getting lectured to as Perot did when questioned about teen pregnancy ("Stop irresponsible sex,' he said emphatically. "Just remember everytime you start thinking about it that Ross said you're not a rabbit.") and drug abusers ("You're a burden to society, and you're selfish.")

Whether it was his MTV appearance or his late night sax playing on the Arsenio Hall show, Clinton won the election with a decisive victory. He broke the Republican hold on the White House while garnering half the 18-29 year-old vote that turned out in numbers much higher than the previous election.

> I think everyone here knows that MTV had a lot to do with the Clinton/Gore victory.
>
> —PRESIDENT BILL CLINTON

MOTOR VOTER

Once in office, Clinton signed the National Voter Registration Act of 1993 (the Motor Voter Act) into law, which became effective on Jan. 1, 1995. The law made voter registration more accessible by providing increased ways citizens could register to vote, including at state departments of motor vehicles. In March 1991, at the urging of Rock the Vote, the rock band R.E.M. had driven a push for the legislation by encouraging fans to request their senators support the Motor Voter bill by mailing in a petition placed on their album *Out of Time*. One month later, Rock the Vote's political director and members of hip hop group KMD delivered a shopping cart filled with the first 10,000 petitions received to a Senate hearing.

In the final round of an MTV audience forum during the 1994 midterm elections, Clinton laid bare the stakes for political discourse once again when his undies became the topic. Responding to a high school student who inquired, "Mr. President, all the world's dying to know: Is it boxers or briefs?", Clinton disclosed, "Mostly briefs."

(A YEAR LATER, IT WAS A CERTAIN WHITE HOUSE INTERN'S UNDIES THAT CAUGHT THE PRESIDENT'S ATTENTION....)

THREE WHITES; TWO STRIPED; ONE ARIZONA RAZORBACKS
(CONTENTS OF BILL CLINTON'S BOYHOOD UNDERWEAR DRAWER, CIRCA 1962)

1996 Bill Clinton v. Robert Dole
Voter Turnout
18-24: 32.4%
total: 54.2%

MTV, working again with Rock the Vote, added a bus adorned with graffiti quotes ranging from Aristotle to Madonna, that traveled the country to its array of voter registration efforts. Whether many young potential voters would hop on board and subsequently turn out at the polls remained unpredictable. Generation X, a more diverse group than ever that shared no seminal unifying experience, initially appeared up for grabs as young voters appeared liberal on social issues and conservative on economic issues. Both campaigns courted the youth vote, with 72-year-old Dole even giving an ol' college try at Animal House-inspired humor. Standing before a crowd of students gathered at the Alpha Delta house at Dartmouth College, he tweaked a line from the 1978 classic frat movie to invoke, "It's time to start voting heavily."

Despite initial estimates of a high young voter turnout, that didn't turn out. Those who did show up, however, doled out bad news to Republicans. Young voters favored Clinton by nearly twenty percentage points over Dole.

POTATO POLITICS

MEET ACTIVIST/POLITICIAN MR. POTATO HEAD.

IN 1996, THE LEAGUE OF WOMEN VOTERS WENT OLD SCHOOL AND ENGAGED MR. POTATO HEAD TO URGE COUCH POTATOES OF ALL AGES TO GET OUT TO THE POLLS.

THIS WASN'T THE FIRST ENTRÉE INTO POLITICS FOR THE SPUD.

HE THREW HIS HAT IN THE RING FOR MAYOR OF BOISE, IDAHO IN 1985. DESPITE HIS PLATFORM OF "DOWN-TO-EARTH PROMISES," HE GOT MASHED, RECEIVING ONLY FOUR VOTES.

A PLAIN OL' POLITICAL POTATO

(SORRY, MR. POTATO HEAD DID NOT RECEIVE AN INVITATION TO APPEAR HERE DUE TO INTELLECTUAL PROPERTY CONCERNS.)

MR. POTATO HEAD IS A TRADEMARK OF HASBRO, INC.

<u>2000 George W. Bush v. Al Gore</u>
<u>Voter Turnout</u>
<u>18-24: 32.3%</u>
<u>total: 54.7%</u>

Even though young voters were civically engaged, volunteering at record rates, they were not too interested in voting in the 2000 election. They did not respond to either Bush or Gore, feeling that despite the now obligatory MTV and late night tv appearances, both candidates lacked charisma and failed to explain the central domestic issues —Medicare, Social Security, and prescription drug costs— in ways relevant to them. Many did respond enthusiastically to Green Party candidate Ralph Nader and his progressive agenda who greeted them at large rallies, "Welcome to the politics of joy and justice!"

Neither joy nor justice were in great abundance for any candidate once returns began to be tallied and the results appeared unclear.

In one of the closest and most controversial elections in American history, youth turnout increased only marginally, with only 28% of 18-20 year olds voting in the 2000 election. Those between 18-29 who did show up split their votes about equally between the two candidates.

How their grandparents and other South Floridians voted remained less than clear. Butterfly ballots used in Palm Beach county that were supposed to improve readability for elderly instead caused confusion. The flawed ballot design led to hand counting and the nation became accustomed to seeing images of election examiners squinting at tiny bits of paper trying to determine the intention underlying a hanging chad.

BUTTERFLY BALLOTS

The Supreme Court finally weighed in. The Court ended the Florida recount, which resulted in Bush gaining the White House by winning Florida by 537 votes. Some claimed that Nader, who won 2.7% of the overall national vote, cost Gore the presidency by siphoning off votes in critical states such as Florida that went to Bush.

Given the issues of ballot design and voting system issues, the Help America Vote Act was enacted in 2002 to help states improve their election procedures and technology.

Meanwhile, another technology had also arrived on the scene. Its presence would soon dominate presidential politics going forward.

THE INTERNET.

2004 George W. Bush v. John Kerry
Voter Turnout
18-24: 41.9%
total: 58.3

At a time when the word blog was still set often off by quotation marks, the Internet had already become an important source of political information. In the 2004 election, former Vermont Gov. and Democratic contender Howard Dean first tapped into the younger generation of voters who embraced the info revolution through online outreach and fundraising. Dean lost the nomination to John Kerry, and much of the youth vote remained up for grabs between Kerry and President Bush. Turnout among young voters rose significantly and much more so than that of the overall electorate. Ultimately, Kerry won 54% of voters under 30, his strongest age based group of support, but lost to Bush.

The 2006 midterm elections showed a 3% increase in the youth vote over 2002, even though no single issue seemed dominant and many young voters were undecided until the final days of campaigning.

2008 Barack Obama v. John McCain
Voter Turnout
18-24: 44.3%
total: 58.2%

No one could have missed young voters in 2008. They showed up on the campaign trail and at the polls from the primary season through the general election. Young voters turned up in numbers not seen since the 1972 election to vote for their preferred candidate, Barack Obama. Obama had taken his message to them through texts and Twitter messaging. They responded to his charismatic message of unity and hope that captured the imagination of a generation whose adolescence coincided with the 9/11 attacks, the Afghanistan and Iraq Wars, and Hurricane Katrina.

Young people powered the Obama campaign volunteer effort and showed up at the polls, giving their candidate a decisive margin over John McCain, whose campaign admittedly did not reach out to them until much later and without as much online engagement. Representing 18% of the electorate, they delivered a 34% margin to Obama, almost double that of the margin between Clinton and Dole in 1996.

> I've been looking forward to this ball for quite some time because, when you look at the history of this campaign, what started out as an improbable journey when nobody gave us a chance was carried forward, was inspired by, was energized by young people all across America," he told the room, as supporters shouted, "Yes, we can!" ...
>
> ... And so a new generation inspired a previous generation and that's how change happens in America.
>
> —PRESIDENT BARACK OBAMA

Two years later, Facebook got involved in an election. *(REALLY, THEY ACKNOWLEDGED IT.)* In a study involving 61 million Facebook users during the 2010 midterms, online activity, particularly the influence of close friends, translated to significant real world political behavior. Those users who were shown a message reminding them to vote, together with photos of their friends who had clicked the "I Voted" button were 4% more likely to vote compared to a group that received a voting reminder without a photo and to a control group that did not receive any message. That difference amounted to approximately 340,000 additional votes.

HMMM.... SOCIAL NETWORKS MIGHT AFFECT AN ELECTION?? WONDER WHO ELSE MIGHT HAVE READ THAT REPORT...

2012 Barack Obama v. Mitt Romney
Voter Turnout
18-24: 38.0%
total: 56.5%

Again, in 2012, young voters selected Obama, this time by a 24% margin over Mitt Romney, and representing 19% of the voters. Both campaigns had reached out over the internet and social media, as well as through door-to-door personal contact to attract college students as well as working-class young adults. They showed up, but in fewer numbers and with a little less excitement amidst an economic downturn. Disillusionment with the economy provided an opportunity for Republicans to gain support.

Perhaps that souring mood contributed to a significant decline in the youth vote from the 2008 election. Billionaire and future unsuccessful 2020 Democratic nominee Tom Steyer stepped down from his investment business and up to the task of fighting climate change and mobilizing young people to vote. He founded NextGen Climate (renamed NextGen America in 2017) that reports registering 1.3 million voters since its founding.

In the 2014 midterm elections, pundits noticed that only 23% of young people voted, while 87% of millennials had donated to a charity that year. In addition to the souring economic mood and general feeling of disengagement with the political system, two other factors may have contributed to the decline in voting. The first seemed a throwback to an earlier ugly era, and the second a harbinger of things to come.

First, voter suppression efforts had been on the rise, and many of these particularly affected younger voters. At least 22 states had passed more restrictive voting laws between 2010 and 2014, including barring student identification cards and prohibiting out-of-precinct voting and same day registration.

Minority voters of all ages also faced more obstacles. The Supreme Court decision on June 25, 2013 in *Shelby County v. Holder* made it easier for states to threaten minority voting rights by invalidating key provisions of the Voting Rights Act of 1965 that had required localities with a history of discriminatory voting laws to "preclear" with the federal government proposed changes to voting and election systems. This loss of protection gave rise to many states passing voting laws that adversely affected the ability of voters of color to cast ballots.

Second, the rise of Big Data came at the expense of the little voter. Campaigns began relying more on targeted campaigning where likely and swing voters were seen as more significant than young people who were more difficult to reach since they were less likely to have voting records, a permanent address, or even a landline. Young voters were being criticized as narcissistic, materialistic, and apathetic at the same time they were being ignored and even excluded.

2016 Donald Trump v. Hillary Clinton
Voter Turnout
18-24: 39.4%
total: 56.0%

The youth turnout in 2016 edged up slightly from 2012 level, and represented the only age group whose turnout increased from the prior presidential election. Clinton won 55% of the youth vote, compared to 37% for Trump, who won more younger voters than suggested by pre-election polls.

Trump's strength among young voters came from whites, evangelicals and rural voters whose concerns mirrored his campaign themes that included the state of the country, immigration, and distrust of Clinton. Clinton drew young support from unmarried women and non-whites, but lacked the broad support of young males and white moderates who had backed Pres. Obama in the previous election. Collectively, young voters seemed more independent and less likely to identify with parties.

Former Pres. Obama himself had tried through various late night television appearances to appeal to young voters to turn out to vote for Clinton. On "Full Frontal," he and host Samantha Bee, who posed as a millennial, poked fun at stereotypes that portrayed young people obsessed with social media. Pres. Obama told Bee, "Young people have a bigger stake in this election than anybody. I would hope that you'd be willing to take about the same amount of time that you spend just looking through cat videos on your phone to make sure that the democracy's working."

"SORRY, I WAS JUST SNAPCHATTING MYSELF
AS A BOTTLENOSE DOLPHIN."

Young voters paused from taking selfies and made a difference in several key races, giving an edge to their preferred candidate to capture electoral college votes. Meanwhile, two million young people opted for third-party candidates or chose not to vote for anyone on the ballot. Libertarian candidate Gary Johnson and Green Party candidate Jill Stein attracted many young voters as did the campaign's oldest contender, Sen. Bernie Sanders, who energized many Millennials during the primary season with his progressive agenda. This bloc may have drawn support away from Clinton, much in the way that Nader's 2000 bid was seen to cut into support for Gore.

How foreign interference in this election may have particularly affected the youth vote is not certain, but they comprised part of the audience that witnessed fake news on social media.

AND THEN THINGS CHANGED.

CYNICISM THAT HAD HELPED PUSH YOUNG PEOPLE AWAY FROM THE VOTING BOOTH NOW SPURRED THEM TOWARDS IT.

THE CATALYST WAS CATASTROPHE.

2018: THE YEAR YOUTH TURNED OUT

On Feb. 14, 2018, 17 people were killed and another 17 were injured by an assailant with a semi-automatic rifle at Marjory Stoneman Douglas High School in Parkland, Florida. In the days immediately following, students at the school organized Never Again MSD, a political action committee that advocates for tighter regulations to prevent gun violence.

In that moment, teens showed truth to power and demonstrated their capabilities to make change. They immediately began pressuring politicians to enact gun safety legislation. Three weeks later, due in large part to their activism, Florida enacted the state's most aggressive gun control measures in decades.

> You made your voices heard. You didn't let up. And, you fought until there was change. You helped change our state. You made a difference.
>
> —FLORIDA GOVERNOR RICK SCOTT

They rallied others to join their cause and on Mar. 24 staged the nationwide March For Our Lives, one of the largest protests in U.S. history. Urging a non-partisan approach to support legislation to prevent gun violence, they highlighted the importance of voting to achieve change.

> Stand for us or beware. The voters are coming...
>
> The march is not the climax of this movement, it is the beginning.
>
> —CAMERON KASKY, CO-FOUNDER NEVER AGAIN MSD

In September, Parkland survivors embarked on a multi-city voter registration drive. The emphasis on the ballot continued as high school students nationwide participated in a "Walkout to Vote" in November to protest inaction on gun violence.

> We're making voting something that isn't just checking a box. It's literally you being a hero and you saving lives.
>
> —MATT DEITSCH, MARCH FOR OUR LIVES CHIEF STRATEGIST

On Sept. 25, National Voter Registration Day, a record 800,000 people from all age groups registered. Certainly, voter registration efforts by new and established groups continued. Among them, MTV initiated a new project, +1 The Vote, that highlighted young people using social media messaging and tools to convince their friends to register. Celebrity endorsements also proved effective. After Taylor Swift urged her Instagram followers to get out the vote, approximately 65,000 young people registered within the next 24 hours.

The difference now from prior election cycles was that celebrities now not only included rock stars but youth themselves. Over and over again, young people emphasized the connection between activism, voting, and impact. Their peers listened.

YOUTH REGISTERED IN DROVES AND UPENDED THE 2018 MIDTERMS.

Youth voter turnout increased in every single state from the 2014 midterms and made the difference in several hotly contested state races. In 32 of 34 states, youth turnout increased by at least 7 percentage points, and in 27 of them it increased by double digits. By a historic 35% margin, they favored Democrats over Republicans in House races.

VOTING HAD BECOME COOL.
AND, AS ALWAYS, CRITICAL.

AND NOW

The very first bill introduced by the House in 2019 calls for the expansion of voting rights along with campaign finance reform and the strengthening of governmental ethics. The For The People Act of 2019 includes creating a national voter registration program, restricting the purging of voting rolls, restoring the full protections of the Voting Rights Act of 1965, reinstating felony voting rights, replacing partisan gerrymandering, improving election security, and making Election Day a federal holiday. The bill would alleviate many of the issues faced by young voters by authorizing most colleges to serve as voter registration places, allowing same day and automatic voter registration, and permitting 16 and 17-year-olds to pre-register to vote.

The bill passed the House in March 2019 but Senate Majority Leader Mitch McConnell (R-KY) refuses to allow a vote by the Senate on the legislation. Why? "Because I get to decide what we vote on," remarked Sen. McConnell, who then claimed that people were flooding to the polls.

Notwithstanding any such supposed stampede, many young people attempting to vote have been tripped up in recent years by obstacles placed in their paths to the voting booth. Although the number of college students voting doubled between 2014 and 2018, some states are doubling down on voter suppression tactics. Students are particularly affected by early voting restrictions, onerous identification rules and eligibility issues, and a lack of polling places on college campuses.

WILL THAT STOP YOU FROM TRYING?

NAH, DIDN'T THINK SO.

BUT YOU NEED TO TRY HARDER.

In the 2020 presidential primary season, many young voters did not show up to vote. It's not that they weren't motivated. Despite eliciting enthusiasm from young voters attracted to his progressive platform, Sen. Bernie Sanders (D-VT) did not receive many of their actual votes. No one else did either. To be clear, young voters did overwhelmingly cast their ballots for Sanders, but there just weren't that many of them who showed up. They had stayed home again—even before the stay-at-home orders warranted by the COVID-19 pandemic. Although overall turnout exceeded that in 2016, the youth vote was flat or down in many states. Exit polls conducted on Super Tuesday reveal that those younger than 30 did not participate at a rate over 20% in the 14 states that held Democratic primaries that day. No comparable analysis can be made regarding Republican primaries as the top of the ticket was not at stake.

Regardless of how one's political sensibilities align, one has to actually vote to make a difference.

An **enduring truth of politics** is that, whether in presidential years or midterm races, younger voters consistently turn out at a lower rate than older ones. (The 18-29 year olds trail the 30-44-year-olds, who trail the 45-59- year-olds. Voters 60 and up are the Election Day rock stars.) Until that changes, young people will have a tough time getting their concerns taken as seriously as they deserve.

-New York Times Editorial Board, April 12, 2020

IV. WILL YOU?

WHY VOTE?

So here we are. Whether you show up to vote in the next election is up to you.

It comes down to this:
Do you want to strengthen democracy?
Do you want to shape history?
Do you want to shape the future?
Do you want to be counted now?
What will it be?
What will YOU do?

Every vote matters. It might be **YOURS** that decides an election.

In just the last twenty years, over a dozen elections were decided by a single vote or ended in a tie. In 2000, Pres. Bush won the White House by a margin of 537 votes out of nearly 6 million cast. In 2016, Pres. Trump won the Electoral College by a margin of less than 80,000 votes out of approximately 13.7 million cast in three states.

> **Those who stay away from the election think that one vote will do no good. 'Tis but one step more to think one vote will do no harm.**
>
> **—Ralph Waldo Emerson**

As it has in the past, the youth vote can make a significant difference. And it will matter again. It may not provide the decisive margin every time, or even be on the side that wins, but Americans between 18 and 23 will account for one-in-ten eligible voters in the 2020 presidential election.

GEN Z ON THE MARCH

Your vote can impact some of the most pressing issues facing your generation: racial equality, social justice, climate change, income inequality, public health, education, school safety, the national debt, personal debt, housing costs, national security, and more. Democracy itself needs your participation.

A national spring 2020 poll of Americans between ages 18 and 29 conducted by the Harvard Public Opinion Project found that COVID-19 and healthcare concerns topped their issues. Prior to the pandemic, the economy and the environment had been the focus of their attention, according to the group's fall 2019 data.

> **More than three-in-five (61%) young Americans, and 75% of likely voters agree that the outcome of the 2020 presidential election will make a difference in their lives**
>
> **-HARVARD YOUTH POLL, SPRING 2020**

The next poll will likely reveal systemic racism and inequality at the top of the list. Following the killing of George Floyd, an unarmed Black man, at the hands of Minneapolis police on May 25, protests erupted throughout the country calling for an end to police brutality, racism, and inequality. Thousands of Americans of all ages and races marched to voice their frustrations and anger.

Non-violent civil disobedience is a powerful tool to raise awareness and galvanize support. But that alone is not enough. In order to translate protest into policy, show up to cast your ballot, and not just every four years for presidential elections. State and local elections matter greatly. Those contests result in selecting the officials most responsible for such matters as local law enforcement and populating the state houses that typically determine voting districts and rules.

You are the most racially and ethnically diverse generation of Americans ever. Whether your vote aligns with the majority of your peers or not, quite simply, you may find yourself on the losing side. That doesn't mean you should get out of the game.

> **Always vote for principle, though you may vote alone, and you may cherish the sweetest reflection that your vote is never lost.**
>
> **-PRESIDENT JOHN QUINCY ADAMS**

ARE THERE PROBLEMS WITH VOTING?

YOU BETCHA'.

Election security, gerrymandering, campaign finance all need attention.

THE VERY ACT OF VOTING FACES CHALLENGES.

Voter suppression is very real. New methods have replaced the prohibited twentieth century Jim Crow tactics of poll taxes and literacy tests to hinder voting. Twenty-first century tactics target minority and lower income communities and include extreme partisan gerrymandering, restrictive voter identification rules, and limiting access to polling stations. Similar roadblocks to suppress college students from voting are on the rise. Public health concerns in light of COVID-19 also raise issues regarding in-person voting and shine a spotlight on the need for both mail-in ballots and the protection of the U.S. Postal Service.

None of these things are good for democracy but they will only get worse if you don't care. That's what neglecting to or deciding not to vote shows, whether you intend that as your message or not.

> But in this country we have one great privilege which they don't have in other countries. When a thing gets to be absolutely unbearable the people can rise up and throw it off. That's the finest asset we've got—the ballot box.
>
> —MARK TWAIN

> Nobody will ever deprive the American people of the right to vote except the American people themselves - and the only way to do this is by not voting at all.
>
> —PRESIDENT FRANKLIN D. ROOSEVELT

Our American heritage is threatened as much by our own indifference as it is by the most unscrupulous office or by the most powerful foreign threat. The future of this Republic is in the hands of the American voter.

—President Dwight D. Eisenhower

You could choose to sit an election out and quit.

But is that what America was founded for?

Or what the Founding Fathers would do?

Or Susan B. Anthony?

Or Martin Luther, King, Jr.?

Is that what those who gave their lives to protect American democracy would do?

Not likely.

Someone struggled for your right to vote. Use it.

—Susan B. Anthony

HERE'S HOW

See Appendix D for information about registering to vote and voting logistics.

ONE MORE THING

"You're off to great places!" you've heard quite a lot.

Make the voting booth a regular stop at every age. Even when you get old and grey.

"OH, THE PLACES YOU'LL GO!"

That's what 106-year-old evangelical music and ramen soup lovin' Haitian immigrant Desilene Victor did.

She voted in three U.S. presidential elections, beginning at age almost-98 in 2008 when she first became eligible after obtaining her citizenship.

When she set off to vote in her Miami neighborhood in 2012, she had no idea of the place she'd eventually go because of her act of civic conscience. That place was the Capitol and a standing ovation at the 2013 State of the Union address by President Obama who acknowledged her steadfast determination to cast her ballot. Her special recognition resulted from what should have been a simple act- the attempt to vote.

The nearly 102-year old had waited in line under the hot Florida sun for three hours to vote at her local library before being advised to come back later. That didn't dissuade her from returning that evening to cast her ballot, even though no poll workers could assist her in her native Creole language despite the community's large Haitian population.

> No one should have to wait in line that long. But I was going to persist because I really wanted to vote.
>
> —DESILENE VICTOR

Nor did anything deter her from sending a letter to Justice Antonin Scalia in March 2013 criticizing his opinion voiced during oral arguments in *Shelby County v. Holder* that the Voting Rights Act represents the "perpetuation of racial entitlement."

> Justice Scalia, the Voting Rights Act is not a racial entitlement. It is an important protection that helps all Americans exercise their right to vote. It was put in place because, sadly, there are people in this country who don't want everyone to have an equal voice at the ballot box.
>
> Equality and the right to vote are the shining lights of American democracy that drew me to these shores, and that right should not be taken away. In fact, it should be made stronger to help more voters who faced obstacles like I did.
>
> —DESILENE VICTOR

Nor did anything deter her from voting in 2016.

> Vote, vote, vote. (translated from Creole, "Voter, voter, voter")
>
> —DESILENE VICTOR

HAT WORN BY DESILENE VICTOR
TO VOTE IN 2016 PRESIDENTIAL ELECTION

Victor understood a thing or two about the importance of voting as the foundation of American democracy.

So did Ben Franklin.

Following the signing of the Constitution, when asked whether Americans now had a republic or a monarchy, he reportedly replied, "A republic, if you can keep it."

20/20 FOR 2020

A REPUBLIC

DEFINITION:

1 A
_____

(1): A GOVERNMENT HAVING A CHIEF OF STATE WHO IS NOT A MONARCH AND WHO IN MODERN TIMES IS USUALLY A PRESIDENT

(2): A POLITICAL UNIT (SUCH AS A NATION) HAVING SUCH A FORM OF GOVERNMENT

B
_____

(1): A GOVERNMENT IN WHICH SUPREME POWER RESIDES IN A BODY OF CITIZENS ENTITLED TO VOTE AND IS EXERCISED BY ELECTED OFFICERS AND REPRESENTATIVES RESPONSIBLE TO THEM AND GOVERNING ACCORDING TO LAW

(2): A POLITICAL UNIT (SUCH AS A NATION) HAVING SUCH A FORM OF GOVERNMENT

C
_____

A USUALLY SPECIFIED REPUBLICAN GOVERNMENT OF A POLITICAL UNIT

WILL <u>YOU</u> KEEP IT?

APPENDIX A

TEXT OF 26TH AMENDMENT

Amendment XXVI to the U.S. Constitution

Passed by Congress on Mar. 23, 1971. Ratified July 1, 1971.

Section 1.

The right of citizens of the United States, who are eighteen years of age or older, to vote shall not be denied or abridged by the United States or by any State on account of age.

Section 2.

The Congress shall have power to enforce this article by appropriate legislation.

APPENDIX B

RATIFICATION OF 26TH AMENDMENT

(states listed alphabetically on date of ratification)

Connecticut, March 23, 1971

Delaware, March 23, 1971

Minnesota, March 23, 1971

Tennessee, March 23, 1971

Washington, March 23, 1971

Hawaii, March 24, 1971

Massachusetts, March 24, 1971

Montana, March 29, 1971

Arkansas, March 30, 1971

Idaho, March 30, 1971

Iowa, March 30, 1971

Nebraska, April 2, 1971

New Jersey, April 3, 1971

Kansas, April 7, 1971

Michigan, April 7, 1971

Alaska, April 8, 1971

Maryland, April 8, 1971

Indiana, April 8, 1971

Maine, April 9, 1971

Vermont, April 16, 1971

Louisiana, April 17, 1971

California, April 19, 1971

Colorado, April 27, 1971

Pennsylvania, April 27, 1971

Texas, April 27, 1971

South Carolina, April 28, 1971

West Virginia, April 28, 1971

New Hampshire, May 13, 1971

Arizona, May 14, 1971

Rhode Island, May 27, 1971

New York, June 2, 1971

Oregon, June 4, 1971

Missouri, June 14, 1971

Wisconsin, June 22, 1971

Illinois, June 29, 1971

Alabama, June 30, 1971

Ohio, June 30, 1971

North Carolina, July 1, 1971

Oklahoma, July 1, 1971

Virginia, July 8, 1971

Wyoming, July 8, 1971

Georgia, October 4, 1971

South Dakota, March 4, 2014

WHEREFORE ART THOU, FLORIDA, KENTUCKY, MISSISSIPPI, NEVADA, NEW MEXICO, NORTH DAKOTA, UTAH?

APPENDIX C

A LITTLE 26TH AMENDMENT TIMELINE

1788   Constitution ratified; silent on voting age; states determine voting qualifications; most continue colonial practice of restricting voting to white male property owners aged 21 and older

1820   working class white males begin to demand vote; Missouri state convention defeats measure to lower voting age

1821   New York state convention debates linkage between conscription and voting age; extends suffrage to males over 20 who served in military in addition to those owning property

1830   most states by now abandon property and income voting qualifications for white males

1867   New York state convention rejects lowering voting age to native-born white males between 18 and 21

1868   Fourteenth Amendment ratified-provides for reduction of representation if states deny vote to males 21 and older and gives Congress right to enforce provisions by legislation

1870   Fifteenth Amendment ratified-prohibits denial of right to vote on basis of race

1920   Nineteenth Amendment ratified-prohibits denial of vote on basis of sex

1939   17% of Americans favor lowering voting age to 18 in first Gallup poll on issue

1941   Sen. Harley Kilgore (D-WV) offers amendment to lower voting age to 18 by constitutional amendment

1942   U.S. military draft age lowered to 18; Rep. Victor Wickersham (D-OK) offers constitutional amendment to lower voting age in federal elections to 18; Sen. Arthur Vandenberg (R-MI) and Rep. Jennings Randolph (D-WV) offer constitutional amendment to lower voting age to 18; Sen. Vandenberg's text (S.J. Res. 166) text forms basis of eventual 26th Amendment

1943   First Lady Eleanor Roosevelt and NEA endorse 18-year-old voting; "old enough to fight, old enough to vote" slogan gains popularity; Georgia ratifies lowering state voting age to 18; over 40 resolutions in 30 other states fail

1946-64 U.S. baby boom

1952   Edward Kuekes' Pulitzer Prize-winning cartoon "Aftermath" (commenting on irony of young U.S. soldiers drafted to fight in Korean War but unable to vote) published in Cleveland *Plain Dealer*

1954   Pres. Dwight Eisenhower becomes first president to call for constitutional amendment lowering voting age to 18 during State of Union address; resolution proposing constitutional amendment to lower voting age to 18 in federal and state elections defeated in first vote on issue by full Senate

1954   Territory of Guam lowers voting age to 18

1955-73 escalation of U.S. role in Vietnam War

1955   Kentucky lowers voting age to 18

1959   Alaska and Hawaii becomes states with respective voting ages set at 19 and 20

1960   American Samoa sets voting age to 20

1961   Twenty-Third Amendment ratified-grants District of Columbia residents right to vote in presidential elections

1963   President's Commission on Registration and Voter Participation recommends states consider lowering voting age to 18

1964   Twenty-Fourth Amendment ratified-prohibits poll taxes in federal elections; Trust Territories of the Pacific set 18 as minimum voting age

1965   Voting Rights Act of 1965 bans racial discrimination in voting; American Samoa lowers voting age to 18

1966   *Harvard Law Review* publishes Prof. Archibald Cox's article that provides basis for claiming voting age could be reduced by statute

1968   Pres. Johnson calls on Congress to lower the age to 18; *New York Times* reverses stance and supports lowering age; college students form Let Us Vote (LUV); college students power Sen. Eugene McCarthy (D-MN) presidential campaign; social unrest on rise

1969   Youth Franchise Coalition, an umbrella group of national civil rights and educational organizations, formed to lobby federal and state legislature; NAACP Youth and College Division holds mobilization conference; approximately 60 resolutions introduced in Congress to lower voting age to 18; Alaska lowers voting age to 18; presidential commission investigating violence in society recommends reducing voting age to 18

1970   Congress passes and Pres. Nixon signs extension of Voting Rights Act that includes rider reducing voting age to 18 in all elections; Supreme Court reviews suits regarding voting age provisions and holds in *Oregon v. Mitchell* that voting age provisions valid only for federal elections; decision results in some states having bifurcated voting rolls for federal and state/local elections

1971   Congress approves in March proposed constitutional amendment to lower voting age to 18 and sends to states to ratify; Twenty-sixth Amendment ratified July 1; certified as valid on July 5.

APPENDIX D

HOW TO REGISTER AND VOTE

Registration and voting logistics are subject to change, especially in light of COVID-19, which highlights the need for mail-in voting.

Regardless of the mechanics of actual voting, you first need to register. You can also get involved with numerous organizations to help get others registered and excited about voting. **If you have a question about the voting process or experience a problem registering or voting, you can contact the national nonpartisan Election Protection coalition at 866-OUR-VOTE.**

REGISTER:

TIMING MATTERS. REGISTER AS SOON AS POSSIBLE IN ORDER TO BE ELIGIBLE TO VOTE AT THE NEXT ELECTION.

Voter registration itself shouldn't take much time but needs to be timely. States set their registration requirements and deadlines.

Yes, you can register to vote at your college address!

The U.S. Election Assistance Commission (http://eac.gov/), established by the Help America Vote Act of 2002, is an independent bipartisan commission that provides key dates and information for registering and voting for each state. Contact your state election office or the Election Protection coalition if you need more information.

U.S. citizens can use the National Mail Voter Registration Form to register, update registration information regarding any name or address change, or to register with a political party. The form is downloadable in fifteen languages. You must follow state-specific instructions listed for your state beginning on page three of the form and listed alphabetically; sign as indicated and mail according to instructions. The form can be found on the EAC's website, at https://www.eac.gov/voters/national-mail-voter-registration-form

Remember to update your registration as soon as possible if your name has changed, if you have moved, or if you wish to register with a political party. Confirm your registration if you're not sure whether you've already done so or not sure if your information is up-to-date.

VOTE:

Even if you can register to vote online, you cannot currently vote online in federal elections. You either need to vote in person at an official polling place or by absentee ballot or mail-in ballot, as permitted. Some states also allow early voting.

Check the deadlines and requirements for all forms of voting.

Locate your polling place and hours of operation ahead of time. Find out what forms of identification you need to bring with you. The national nonpartisan organization VoteRiders (www.voteriders.org) can answer questions about voter IDs.

First time voters who did not register in person or show ID at time of registration must show identification prior to voting.

Most states require you to bring certain kinds of identification with you when you show up to vote. Typically, photo IDs such as driver's licenses, state-issued ID cards, military ID cards, and U.S. passports are acceptable. Some states accept birth certificates, Social Security cards, bank statements, and utility bills.

ALL ELECTIONS MATTER:

Register and vote in every state and local election, not just the presidential ones. You can have a hand in making policies like revenue measures, as well as selecting your state and federal representatives, your local law enforcement officials, your local school board, and possibly even your animal control officer. Just ask your pal Fido if he thinks that's important.

SHOW OFF:

TELL YOUR FRIENDS.
TELL YOUR MOM.
TELL YOUR HIGH SCHOOL HISTORY TEACHER.
TELL THE WORLD.

CELEBRATE:

HAVE A PARTY. EAT CAKE. (SEE APPENDIX E).

APPENDIX E

MAKE AMERICA CAKE AGAIN

Marie Antoinette may have faced unpalatable consequences from supposedly dismissing the plight of her subjects by suggesting "Let them eat cake," but that was in Revolutionary France. In Revolutionary America, people feasted on cake to celebrate Election Day.

During military training days, colonists made "great cakes" to serve to militia members called upon for training sessions. At least as early as 1771, these cakes were part of Election Day celebrations. That year, the Connecticut General Assembly provided the funds for the ingredients for a large cake. In fact, Hartford takes the cake for having its name attached to early recipes for this American baked good. After the Revolution, Election Day festivities typically included copious amounts of food and drink, often served at town meetings or outside polling places.

In 1796, Amelia Simmons included a recipe in her book, *American Cookery*, the first cookbook by an American to be published in the United States.

> Election cake—Thirty quarts flour, 10 pound butter, 14 pound sugar, 12 pound raisins, 3 dozen eggs, one pint wine, one quart brandy, 4 ounces cinnamon, 4 ounces fine colander seed, 3 ounces ground allspice; wet flour with milk to the consistence of bread over night, adding one quart yeast; the next morning work the butter and sugar together for half an hour, which will

> render the cake much lighter and whiter; when it has risen light work in every other ingredient except the plumbs, which work in when going into the oven.
>
> —AMELIA SIMMONS, *AMERICAN COOKERY*

IT'S HARD TO NOT GET EXCITED ABOUT CAKE.
EVEN AN EXTRAORDINARILY DENSE ONE.

In the young United States, Election Day remained a significant holiday. It often took time for people to reach polling places and to count the votes. People got hungry. Making the cakes also provided women with an outlet to express their civic spirit while they were excluded from voting. By 1830, Hartford housewives based their reputations on the quality of their huge cakes, often weighing about 12 pounds each.

Over time, Election Day traditions faded out.

Election Cake crumbled into oblivion.

Then, in 2016, under the leadership of Susannah Gebhart, baker and co-owner of Old World Levain Bakery in Asheville, North Carolina, professional foodies, home bakers, and others joined forces in a non-partisan nation-wide venture to raise awareness about our culinary heritage and to generate funds for greater voter access and rights. Culinary arts professor and author Richard Miscovich devised a base recipe from researching historical recipes and coined the project's hashtag. You can find out more and discover adaptations of the recipe by searching the hashtag #makeamericacakeagain.

IT SURE SOUNDS A LOT BETTER THAN TURTLE SOUP.

NOTES

Epigraph

New York Times-"Sitting this election out": "Hey Kids: Get Out There and Vote!" *New York Times*, Apr. 12, 2020, E 12. https://www.nytimes.com/2020/04/12/opinion/biden-sanders-young-voters.html?searchResultPosition=1 .

Preface

Mitchell, "The more votes cast": William C. Mitchell, *"Why Vote?"* (Chicago: Markham Publishing Company, 1971), 19.

I. Should They?

Early America

"a little dance": ____, "Ben Franklin's Two Birthdays," The Franklin Institute, https://www.fi.edu/benjamin-franklin/happy-birthday-ben-franklin (accessed Jun. 30, 2020). According to this article, Franklin's birthday became Jan. 17 due to Great Britain's switch to the Gregorian calendar in 1752 although he was born in Boston on Jan. 6, 1706.

Illustration, "Miniature Children": See David, Joanna, and Abigail Mason, 1670, oil on canvas painting attributed to the Freake-Gibbs Painter (American, active 1670). Fine Arts Museums of San Francisco, Gift of Mr. and Mrs. John D. Rockefeller 3rd. https://www.famsf.org/blog/meet-de-young-family ; https://commons.wikimedia.org/wiki/File:%27David,_Joanna,_and_Abigail_Mason%27_by_the_Freake-Gibbs_Limner.JPG .

Brent-"I've come to seek": Joyce Appleby, Eileen Chang, and Neva Goodwin, eds., *Encyclopedia of Women in American History, Volume 1, Colonization, Revolution, and the New Nation, 1585-1820* (Armonk, NY: Sharpe Reference, 2002), 57.

Hamilton-"If it were probable": Alexander Hamilton, The Farmer Refuted, or A more impartial and comprehensive View of the Dispute between Great-Britain and the Colonies,(New York, 1775), in Harold C. Syrett, ed., *The Papers of Alexander Hamilton* (New York: Columbia University Press, 1961-1979),1:81-165, https://www.dhr.history.vt.edu/modules/us/mod03_rev/evidence_detail_13.html.

Abigail Adams-"Remember the Ladies": Abigail Adams to John Adams, 31 Mar. - 5 Apr. 1776 [electronic edition]. Adams Family Papers: An Electronic Archive. Massachusetts Historical Society, http://www.masshist.org/digitaladams/.

John Adams-"Such is the Frailty": John Adams to James Sullivan, 26 May 1776, Founders Online, National Archives, version of January 18, 2019, https://founders.archives.gov/documents/Adams/06-04-02-0091. [Original source: *The Adams Papers, Papers of John Adams, vol. 4, Feb.–Aug. 1776*, ed. Robert J. Taylor. Cambridge, MA: Harvard University Press, 1979, 208–13.

Franklin-"Some of the greatest rogues": Michael Waldman, "The Right to Vote? Don't Count on It," Feb. 29, 2016, Brennan Center For Justice, https://www.brennancenter.org/our-work/analysis-opinion/right-vote-dont-count-it.

Franklin-"Today a man": Alexander Keyssar, *The Right to Vote: The Contested History of Democracy in the United States* (New York: Basic Books, 2000), 3 (citing to Benjamin Franklin, *The Casket, or Flowers of Literature, Wit and Sentiment* (1828)).

U.S. Constitution- "The electors": U.S. Const. art. I, sec. 2.

1800s-early 1900s

Van Buren-"And the question": Nathan H. Carter and William L. Stone, *Reports of the Proceedings and Debates of the Constitutional Convention of 1821*, Assembled for the Purpose of Amending the Constitution of the State of New York (Albany: E. and E. Hosford, 1821), 257.

Kent-"That extreme democratic principle": Carter and Stone, *Reports of the Proceedings*, 220.

"Nothing said American democracy like turtle soup.": See Jack Hitt, "What Ever Happened to Turtle Soup?" *Saveur*, Oct. 14, 2015. https://www.saveur.com/history-of-turtle-soup-hunting/

de Tocqueville-"baffled by": Alexis de Tocqueville to his mother, May 14, 1831 in *Letters from America* (trans. By Frederick Brown) (New Haven: Yale University Press, 2010) in https://hudsonreview.com/2013/03/letters-from-america/#.XqCGTS2ZP1I.

de Tocqueville-"When a nation": Alexis de Tocqueville, *Democracy in America*, Chapter IV: The Principle Of The Sovereignty Of The People In America, (Henry Reeve, transl.),Project Gutenberg, last updated 2013, https://www.gutenberg.org/files/815/815-h/815-h.htm#link2HCH0008.

Blair-"If these volunteer": Josiah Henry Benton, *Voting in the Field: A Forgotten Chapter of the Civil War* (Boston: Privately Printed, 1915), 96.

Douglass-"Once let the black man": Frederick B. Douglass, Apr. 6, 1863, cited in "Changing America: The Emancipation Proclamation, 1863, and the March on Washington, 1963, National Museum of American History, https://americanhistory.si.edu/changing-america-emancipation-proclamation-1863-and-march-washington-1963/1863/military-service.

Douglass-"I am for": Frederick B. Douglass, "What the Black Man Wants," (speech, Boston, MA , Apr. 1865).

Anthony-"It was we": Susan B. Anthony, "Is it a Crime for a U.S. Citizen to Vote?" (speech, _____, Apr. 3, 1873).

Wilson-"We have made": Woodrow Wilson, "Equal Suffrage," Address of the President of the United States, U.S. Senate, Sept. 30, 1918, (DC: Government Printing Office: 1918), 3 https://www.senate.gov/artandhistory/history/resources/pdf/WilsonSpeech1918.pdf

U.S. Constitution-"Representatives shall be": U.S. Const., amend. XIV, sec. 2.

1940s

Boren, "lie": Lyle Boren, "Congressional speech given by Lyle Boren on the floor ," Remarks, Washington, D.C., January 10, 1940, in John Steinbeck's America, accessed Feb. 28, 2020, http://steinbeck.oucreate.com/items/show/34

Boren, "flatheads"; "They are too young": Rep. Boren, 88 *Congressional Record* 8300 (1942).

Vandenberg, "Mr. President": Sen. Vandenberg, 88 *Congressional Record* 8316 (1942).

Eleanor Roosevelt, "I have noticed": Eleanor Roosevelt, "My Day, January 21, 1943," The Eleanor Roosevelt Papers Digital Edition (2017), accessed Feb. 28, 2019, https://www2.gwu.edu/~erpapers/myday/displaydocedits.cfm?_y=1943&_f=md056400.

Randolph, "I feel": Rep. Randolph, A Joint Resolution Proposing an Amendment to the Constitution of the United States Extending the Right to Vote to Citizens Eighteen Years of Age or Older: Hearing Before Subcommittee No. 1 of the House Committee on the Judiciary, 78th Cong. 3, 10 (1943).

Letter to *New York Times*, "Of all the crackpot": George Washington Williams, "Lowering Voting Age Opposed," Letter to *New York Times*, Aug. 26, 1943.

"Raise Don't Lower the Voting Age": See Rebecca De Schweinitz, Rebecca, "The Proper Age for Suffrage," In *Age in America: The Colonial Era to the Present*, edited by Corinne T. Field and Nicholas L. Syrett, (New York and London: New York University Press, 2015), 209-36.

"old enough to fight, old enough to vote": See "Statement of Hon. Ellis Arnall, Gov. of the State of Georgia," in U.S. Congress, House, Committee on the Judiciary, Subcommittee No. 1, *A Joint Resolution Proposing an Amendment to the Constitution of the United States; Extending the Right to Vote to Citizens Eighteen Years of Age or Older.* 78th Cong., 1st sess., Oct. 20, 1943, 11.

1950s

Edward Kuekes, "Aftermath," *Cleveland Plain Dealer*, Nov. 9, 1952.

Moody, "I remember": Senate Committee on the Judiciary, Subcommittee on Constitutional Amendments, *Proposing an Amendment to the Constitution of the United States to Grant to Citizens of the United States Who Have Attained the Age of Eighteen the Right to Vote: Hearing Before the Subcommittee of the Senate Committee on the Judiciary*, 82d Cong. 61 (1952).

Eisenhower, "For years": Dwight D. Eisenhower, "Annual Message to the Congress on the State of the Union. Jan. 7, 1954," online by Gerhard Peters and John T. Woolley, The American Presidency Project. https://www.presidency.ucsb.edu/node/232936

Truman: "Twenty-one is: George Gallup, "Eighteen-to Twenty-Year-Olds Surpass Adults in Political Quiz," Mar. 2, (reprinted in 100 *Congressional Record*, 6972, (1954)).

Eisenhower, "if I can": ____. "Truman and Eisenhower: When the Man Who Loved Roads Met the Man Who Changed America." Updated June 27, 2017. On U.S. Department of Transportation Federal Highway Administration. https://www.fhwa.dot.gov/infrastructure/met.cfm.

Celler, "Voting is"; "If a person": Rep. Celler, 100 *Congressional Record* 3050 (1954).

Langer, "When I left": Sen. Langer, 100 *Congressional Record* 6957 (1954).

Russell, "I do not": Sen. Russell, 100 *Congressional Record* 6964 (1954).

Dirksen, "if you are": Sen. Dirksen, 100 *Congressional Record* 6972 (1954).

Kennedy, "although the maturity": Sen. Kennedy, 100 Congressional Record 6978 (1954).

Long, "I am entirely": Sen. Long, 100 *Congressional Record* 6978-79 (1954).

New York Times, "poor planning"; "getaway day": C.P. Trussell, "Senate Defeats President's Plan For Voting at 18," May 22, 1954, *New York Times*, p. 1 https://timesmachine.nytimes.com/timesmachine/1954/05/22/issue.html

Fredericks, "I feel that": Gloria Fredericks, "Remarks to the Delegates of the Alaska Constitutional Convention," (speech, Fairbanks, Alaska, Jan. 13, 1956), in "Creating Alaska - The Origins of the 49th State." https://www.alaska.edu/creatingalaska/constitutional-convention/speeches-to-the-conventio/speeches-to-the-conventio/fredericks/

Senate Judiciary Committee, "This country": Senate Committee on the Judiciary, Interim Report: Comic Books and Juvenile Delinquency, 83rd Cong., 1- 2d sess., Mar. 14, 1955, S. Rep. 62.

Georgia lawmaker, "the recent": Jenny Cheng, "How Eighteen-Year-Olds Got the Vote," (Aug. 4, 2016), available at SSRN: https://ssrn.com/abstract=2818730 or http://dx.doi.org/10.2139/ssrn.2818730(fn 134, citing to Albert Riley, Ga. Campuses Alive with Politics as Teen-Age Voters Debate Issues," *Atlanta Journal & Atlanta Constitution*, Oct. 26, 1952, at 1F).

Maryland state senator, "Do you": Cheng, "How Eighteen-Year-Olds," (fn 136, citing to Laurence Stern, "Elvis Helps Kill Bill for Vote at 18," *Washington Post & Herald*, Feb. 27, 1957, at B1.

King, "Give us": Martin Luther King, Jr. "Give Us The Ballot," (speech, Washington, DC, May 17, 1957), on The Martin Luther King, Jr. Research and Education Institute, Stanford University. https://kinginstitute.stanford.edu/king-papers/documents/give-us-ballot-address-delivered-prayer-pilgrimage-freedom.

1960s

Lewis, "The first time": John Lewis, "An Oral History of Selma and the Struggle for the Voting Rights Act," Dec. 25, 2014, *Time*, https://time.com/3647070/selma-john-lewis-voting-rights-act/

King, Martin Luther King, Jr., "Now is the time": Martin Luther King, Jr., "I Have A Dream…," (speech, March on Washington, DC, Aug. 28, 1963), on U.S. National Archives and Records Administration. https://www.archives.gov/files/press/exhibits/dream-speech.pdf

Standard XVI, "Voting by Persons" and discussion of report: Report of the Commission on Voting Participation and Registration, President Lyndon B. Johnson, Washington, DC. Dec. 20, 1963, 43-44.

Malcolm X, "We suffer": Malcolm X, "The Ballot or the Bullet," (speech, King Solomon Baptist Church, Detroit, Michigan, Apr. 12, 1964), on American Public Media. http://americanradioworks.publicradio.org/features/blackspeech/mx.html

Lewis, "I don't know": Lewis, "An Oral History."

Johnson, "There is": Lyndon B. Johnson, "President Johnson's Special Message to the Congress: The American Promise. March 15, 1965," in *Public Papers of the Presidents of the United States: Lyndon B. Johnson, 1965, Volume I*, entry 107, 281-287 (Washington, DC: Government Printing Office, 1966) http://www.lbjlibrary.org/lyndon-baines-johnson/speeches-films/president-johnsons-special-message-to-the-congress-the-american-promise

Johnson, "If you do this": Lyndon B. Johnson, "Remarks on the Signing of the Voting Rights Act, August 6, 1965," Miller Center of Public Affairs, University of Virginia, https://millercenter.org/the-presidency/presidential-speeches/august-6-1965-remarks-signing-voting-rights-act.

re *Wild in the Streets*, "By far, the best American film"; "A very blunt": Renata Adler, "Going 'Wild in the Streets," *New York Times*, June 16, 1968, D1. https://timesmachine.nytimes.com/timesmachine/1968/06/16/91230230.html?pageNumber=117.

re *Wild in the Streets*, "an artifact"; "image of generational megalomania": J. Hoberman, "Are You Over 35? 'Wild in the Streets' Should Scare You," *New York Times*, Sept. 30, 2016. https://www.nytimes.com/2016/10/02/movies/wild-in-the-streets.html?-searchResultPosition=1

Bayh, "This force": Sen. Bayh (D-IN), Senate Committee on the Judiciary, Subcommittee on Constitutional Amendments, *Hearings On S.J. Res. 8, S.J. Res. 14, and S.J. Res. 78 Relating to Lowering the Voting Age to 18*, 90th Cong. 2 (1968).

Javits, "I am convinced": Sen. Javits (R-NY), 1968 Hearings, 11.

Hechler, "Many older": Sen. Hechler (D-WV), 1968 Hearings, 74.

Johnson, "[It is…]": David R. Jones, Johnson Submits Plan for Voting by 18-Year-Olds, *New York Times*, June 28, 1968, at 1.

New York Times, "In a real sense": "Harnessing the Youth Tide," *New York Times*, June 30, 1968, 12 https://timesmachine.nytimes.com/timesmachine/1968/06/30/79941377.html?pageNumber=147.

Agnew, "Once our": Cheng, "How Eighteen-Year-Olds," (fn 229, citing to "Agnew Favors U.S. Vote at 18," *Atlanta Constitution*, Feb. 16, 1969, at 2A.

1970s

Bayh, "What has": Sen. Bayh (D-IN), Senate Committee on the Judiciary, Subcommittee on Constitutional Amendments, Hearings Before the Subcommittee on Constitutional Amendments of the Committee of the Judiciary United States Senate Ninety-First Congress Second Session on S.J. Res. 7, S.J. Res. 19, S.J. Res. 32, S.J. Res. 34, S.J. Res. 38, S.J. Res. 73, S.J. Res. 73, S.J. Res. 87, S.J. Res. 102, S.J. Res. 105, S.J. Res. 141, S.J. Res. 147, 91st Cong., 2d sess., February 16–17, March 9–10, 1970, 3.

Lumley, "We do not": John M. Lumley, Assistant Executive Secretary of the National Education Association, 1970 Hearings, 93.

Kleindienst, "I am not": Richard G. Kleindienst, Deputy Attorney General of the United States, 1970 Hearings, 79.

Rehnquist, "[W]hat is": William H. Rehnquist, Assistant Attorney General, 1970 Hearings, 236.

DiScullo, "legislative procrastination"; "Legislators as a whole": Alan M. DiScullo, Youth Franchise Coalition, 1970 Hearings, 60.

U.S. Constitution: U.S. Const., amend. XIV, sec. 1 (emphasis added)

Parker, "Eureka": Carey Parker, Interview by James Sterling Young, September, 22, 2008, Edward M. Kennedy Oral History Project, Miller Center, University of Virginia, https://www.emkinstitute.org/resources/carey-parker-09-2008 .

"two great tastes": Hallie Lieberman, "Was it Hershey or Reese That Made Peanut Butter Cups Great?", Atlas Obscura, October 27, 2016, https://www.atlasobscura.com/articles/was-it-hershey-or-reese-that-made-peanut-butter-cups-great.

U.S. Constitution: U.S. Const., amend. XIV, sec. 5.

Kennedy: "Just as Congress": Sen. Edward M. Kennedy (D-MA), *1970 Hearings*, 159.

Goldwater, "The voting age": Sen. Barry Goldwater (R-AZ): *1970 Hearings*, 134.

Brown, "The disenfranchisement": James Brown, Jr., National Youth Director, National Association for the Advancement of Colored People, *1970 Hearings*, 150.

Mead, "As long": Dr. Margaret Mead, Professor of Anthropology, Columbia University, *1970 Hearings*, 225.

Pollak, "I strongly endorse": Dean Louis Pollak, Yale Law School, *1970 Hearings*, 250; 251; 263.

Randolph "there is no question": Sen. Jennings Randolph (D-WV), 116 *Cong. Record* 6944 (1970).

Mansfield, "The distinguished Senator": Sen. Mike Mansfield (D-MT), 116 *Cong. Record* 6944 (1970)

Allen, "So, far from": Sen. James Allen (R-AL), 116 *Cong. Record* 20149(1970)

Celler, "[[I] want to point"; "dodo"; "The statutory voting age": Rep. Emanuel Celler (D-NY), 116 *Cong. Record*, 20160-62 (1970).

Andrews, "[T]he Senate amendment": Rep. George W. Andrews (D-AL), 116 *Cong. Record* 20164 (1970).

Fountain (D-NC), "How ridiculous": Rep. Lawrence H. Fountain (D-NC), 116 *Cong. Record* 20174 (1970).

Podell, "This Congress": Rep. Bertram L. Podell (D-NY), 116 *Cong. Record* 20176 (1970)

Robison (R-NY), "There are two": Rep. Howard Robison (R-NY), 116 *Cong. Record* 20191 (1970).

Randall, "If we adopt": Rep. William Randall (D-MO), 116 *Cong. Record* 20194 (1970).

Ford, "This proposition": Rep. Gerald Ford (R-MI), 116 *Cong. Record* 20197 (1970).

Colmer "We might": Rep. William Colmer (D-MS), 116 *Cong. Record* 20197 (1970).

Nixon, "The time": Richard Nixon, Statement of Signing the Voting Rights Act Amendments of 1970, June 22, 1970, *Public Papers of the Presidents of the United States: Richard M. Nixon*, 1970, 195.

Pen Psychology-resignation letter: See Christopher Klein, "The Last Hours of the Nixon Presidency," History.com, updated Aug. 8, 2014 https://www.history.com/news/the-last-hours-of-the-nixon-presidency-40-years-ago (accessed Mar. 3, 2020).

II. COULD THEY?

Nixon, "Despite my misgivings": Richard Nixon, Statement of Signing the Voting Rights Act Amendments of 1970. June 22, 1970, *Public Papers of the Presidents*, 195.

Black, "Since Congress": *Oregon v. Mitchell*, 400 U.S. 112 (1970), 130.

Douglas, "It is a": *Oregon v. Mitchell*, 144.

Brennan, "In sum": *Oregon v. Mitchell*, 280.

Harlan, "the suggestion": *Oregon v. Mitchell*, 212.

Stewart, "A casual reader": *Oregon v. Mitchell*, 282.

Celler, "[A]ny effort": Rep. Emanuel Celler (D-NY), 117 *Cong. Record* 7533 (1971).

Celler, "By offering"; "the fourth coonskin": Marjorie Hunter, "400-to-19 Vote Finishes Action in Congress on Lowering of Age," *New York Times*, Mar. 2, 1971, 1; 26.

"atmosphere of near panic": R. W. Apple Jr., "The States Ratify Full Vote at 18," *New York Times*, July 1, 1971, at 1.

Constitution, "The Congress": U.S. Const., art. V.

Nixon, "Some 11 million": Richard Nixon, Statement About Ratification of the 26th Amendment to the Constitution Online by Gerhard Peters and John T. Woolley, The American Presidency Project, https://www.presidency.ucsb.edu/node/240351

re witnesses, William Ramsey, "26ᵗʰ Amendment Certification- Personal Reflection of the Certification." http://drwmramsey.com/amendment.html (accessed Jun. 28, 2020.

Shapard: "Every time I go": Cassandra Stephenson, "Election Day 2018: Meet the woman who signed the amendment allowing 18-year-olds to vote," *Jackson Sun*, Nov. 6, 2018, https://www.jacksonsun.com/story/news/local/2018/11/06/meet-woman-who-signed-amendment-allowing-18-year-olds-vote/1905213002/.

Nixon, "I wish"; "the punch"; "By the way": Richard Nixon, Remarks at a Ceremony Marking the Certification of the 26th Amendment to the Constitution Online by Gerhard Peters and John T. Woolley, The American Presidency Project, https://www.presidency.ucsb.edu/node/240368

III. WOULD THEY?

Voting percentages: United States Census Bureau. Reported Voting Rates in Presidential Election Years by Selected Characteristics: November 1964 to 2016. {"Table A-9. Reported Voting Rates in Presidential Election Years, by Selected Characteristics: November 1964 to 2016"; included below}, https://www.census.gov/data/tables/time-series/demo/voting-and-registration/voting-historical-time-series.html

Additional sources regarding data and elections appear in Bibliography.

1972

"good karma": "The Youth Vote," *New York Times*, Aug. 21, 1972 at 30, https://timesmachine.nytimes.com/timesmachine/1972/08/21/81956818.html?pageNumber=30 .

1976

Census Bureau Report: U.S. Bureau of the Census, Current Population Reports, Series P-20, No. 322, "Voting and Registration in the Election of November 1976," (Washington DC: U.S. Government Printing Office, 1978), https://www.census.gov/content/dam/Census/library/publications/1978/demo/p20-322.pdf .

1980

additional data: "Briefing: Seeking Youth," *New York Times*, May 19, 1986, at 14, https://timesmachine.nytimes.com/timesmachine/1986/05/19/031286.html?pageNumber=14 .

1984

"Ladies and gentlemen": "The Golden Age of MTV - And Yes, There Was One," NPR, All Things Considered, Nov. 6, 2011, https://www.npr.org/2011/11/06/141991877/the-golden-age-of-mtv-and-yes-there-was-one .

"Does this man like MTV?" Karen de Witt, "MTV Puts the Campaign on Fast Forward," *New York Times*, Feb. 8, 1992, 8. https://www.nytimes.com/1992/02/08/us/the-1992-campaign-media-mtv-puts-the-campaign-on-fast-forward.html?searchResultPosition=29.

1988

62% of voters: Gwen Ifill, "Clinton Goes Eye to Eye with MTV Generation," *New York Times*, June 17, 1992, 22. https://www.nytimes.com/1992/06/17/us/the-1992-campaign-youth-vote-clinton-goes-eye-to-eye-with-mtv-generation.html?searchResultPosition=1.

1992

"If you had"; "boxers or briefs": Eric Ditzian, "Bill Clinton to Barack Obama: MTV's History With Politics," MTV News, October 12, 2010, http://www.mtv.com/news/1649854/bill-clinton-to-barack-obama-mtvs-history-with-politics/.

"teenybopper"; "Stop irresponsible": Jill Lawrence, "Bush, Perot Appear in Taped Interviews on MTV," AP News, Nov. 1, 1992, https://apnews.com/0c5067773012e145e5116e235eef9c30 .

Bill Clinton, "I think everyone": Ditzian, "Bill Clinton to Barack Obama," MTV News, October 12, 2010, http://www.mtv.com/news/1649854/bill-clinton-to-barack-obama-mtvs-history-with-politics/

R.E.M.: 99% Invisible and Whitney Jones. "Why R.E.M.'s Out of Time Is the Most Politically Significant Album in U.S. History," *Slate*, Jul. 25, 2014. http://www.slate.com/blogs/the_eye/2014/07/25/roman_mars_99_percent_invisible_r_e_m_s_out_of_time_is_the_most_politically.html

"boxers or briefs": Ditzian, "Bill Clinton to Barack Obama."

contents of underwear drawer: "1994 White House Correspondents' Dinner," C-SPAN, Apr. 23, 1994 https://www.c-span.org/video/?56320-1/1994-white-house-correspondents-dinner .

1996

"It's time": Katharine Q. Seelye, "A Grand Old Party Animal Tries Courting Young Voters," *New York Times*, Jan. 21, 1996, 1, https://www.nytimes.com/1996/01/21/us/a-grand-old-party-animal-tries-courting-young-voters.html?searchResultPosition=5 .

"down-to-earth": The Eyes Have It in Idaho, Where Mr. Potato Head Is Running for Mayor of Boise," *People*, Nov. 4, 1985, https://people.com/archive/the-eyes-have-it-in-idaho-where-mr-potato-head-is-running-for-mayor-of-boise-vol-24-no-19/ .

2000

"joy and justice": David W. Chen, "In Nader Supporters' Math, Gore Equals Bush, *New York Times*, Oct. 15, 2000, 28.

additional data: Linda Lyons, "Gallup Brain: History of the Youth Vote," Gallup, Jan. 20, 2004, https://news.gallup.com/poll/10348/gallup-brain-history-youth-vote.aspx .

re Florida vote: Ron Elving, "The Florida Recount of 2000: A Nightmare That Goes on Haunting," NPR, Nov. 12, 2018, https://www.npr.org/2018/11/12/666812854/the-florida-recount-of-2000-a-night-mare-that-goes-on-haunting.

2004

54%: Tom Rosentiel, Scott Keeter, Juliana Horowitz, Alec Tyson, "Young Voters in the 2008 Election." Nov. 13, 2008, Pew Research Center. https://www.pewresearch.org/2008/11/13/young-voters-in-the-2008-election/.

3%: "Voting and Registration in the Election of November 2006," U.S. Census Bureau, June 2008, https://www.census.gov/prod/2008pubs/p20-557.pdf .

2008

Barack Obama: "I've been looking forward": Jocelyn Vena, "Barack Obama Tells Youth Ball His 'Improbable Journey' Was 'Energized By Young People," Jan. 20, 2009, MTV News, http://www.mtv.com/news/1603129/barack-obama-tells-youth-ball-his-im-probable-journey-was-energized-by-young-people/ .

margin; 18%: Tom Rosentiel, "Young Voters in the 2008 Election," Pew Research Center, Nov. 13, 2008 https://www.pewresearch.org/2008/11/13/young-voters-in-the-2008-election/ .

Facebook experiment: Zoe Corbyn, "Facebook experiment boosts US voter turn-out," Sept. 12, 2012, nature https://www.nature.com/news/facebook-experi-ment-boosts-us-voter-turnout-1.11401 (accessed Jun. 29, 2020)

2012

24%; 19%: Pew Research Center, "Young Voters Supported Obama Less, But May Have Mattered More," Nov. 26, 2012. https://www.pewresearch.org/poli-tics/2012/11/26/young-voters-supported-obama-less-but-may-have-mattered-more/ .

2014 low turnout; restrictive voting laws; Big Data: ____, "2014 Youth Turnout and Registration Rates Lowest Ever Recorded," Center for Information & Research on Civic Learning and Engagement, Jul. 21, 2015.https://circle.tufts.edu/latest-re-search/2014-youth-turnout-and-registration-rates-lowest-ever-recorded.

23%: Thom File, "Voting in America: A Look at the 2016 Presidential Election." May 10, 2017, U.S. Census Bureau. https://www.census.gov/content/dam/Census/library/publications/2015/demo/p20-577.pdf .

87%: Robbie Couch, "87% Of Millennials Donated To Charity Last Year And You Should Stop Calling Them Selfish: Report," HuffPost, updated Dec. 6, 2017, https://www.huffpost.com/entry/millennials-volunteer-charity-giving_n_5507778.

1.3 million voters: ____. "Who We Are," NextGen America, https://nextgenamerica.org/about-us/ (accessed Jun. 30, 2020).

2016

55%,37%: ____, "Election Night 2016: 24 Million Youth Voted, Most Rejected Trump," Center for Information & Research on Civic Learning and Engagement, Nov. 14, 2016. https://circle.tufts.edu/latest-research/election-night-2016-24-million-youth-voted-most-rejected-trump.

"Young people have"; "Sorry, I was": Bethonie Butler, "President Obama tells 'spooky story' to Samantha Bee: 'Donald Trump could be president,'" Washington Post, Nov. 1, 2016 https://www.washingtonpost.com/news/artsandentertainment/wp/2016/11/01/president-obama-tells-spooky-story-to-samantha-bee-donald-trump-could-be-president/ .

2018

Scott, "You made": Gov. Rick Scott, Prepared Remarks, "Gov. Scott Signs the Marjory Stoneman Douglas High School Public Safety Act," Mar. 9, 2018, https://www.flgov.com/wp-content/uploads/2018/03/MSD.03.09.18.pdf .

Kasky, "Stand for": Tim Hains, "Parkland Student Cameron Kasky: 'Welcome To The Revolution," RealClearPolitics, Mar. 24, 2018, https://www.realclearpolitics.com/video/2018/03/24/parkland_student_cameron_kasky_welcome_to_the_revolution.html?source=post_page————————————-

Deitsch, "We're making": "Parkland Survivors Launch Tour To Register Young Voters And Get Them Out in November," Weekend Edition Saturday, NPR, Jun. 16, 2018, https://www.npr.org/transcripts/620486174.

800,000 registered: Kayla Epstein and Emily Guskin, "Taylor Swift and Rihanna told young people to register. They're doing it, but are they going to actually vote?" Washington Post, Oct. 12, 2018 https://www.washingtonpost.com/politics/2018/10/12/taylor-swift-rihanna-told-young-people-register-theyre-doing-it-are-they-going-actually-vote/?noredirect=on.

Taylor Swift: Annika Reed, "Taylor Swift teaches fans how to vote early in Instagram post," USA Today, Oct. 17, 2018. https://www.usatoday.com/story/life/people/2018/10/17/taylor-swift-teaches-fans-how-vote-early-instagram-post/1668622002/

youth turnout: 2018 Youth Voter Turnout Increased In Every State." Center for Information & Research on Civic Learning and Engagement, Apr. 2, 2019. https://circle.tufts.edu/latest-research/2018-youth-voter-turnout-increased-every-state?utm_source=Tisch+College+Contact+List&utm_campaign=263675b880-EMAIL_CAMPAIGN_2019_04_29_08_27&utm_medium=email&utm_term=0_246da4d028-263675b880-144249329 .

And Now

Congress, House, *For the People Act of 2019*, HR 1, 116th Cong., 1st sess., introduced in House Jan. 3, 2019 https://www.congress.gov/bill/116th-congress/house-bill/1.

McConnell, "Because I": Marianne Levine, "McConnell won't allow vote on election reform bill," Mar. 6, 2019, *Politico*, https://www.politico.com/story/2019/03/06/mcconnell-election-reform-bill-1207702.

Super Tuesday results and "An enduring truth of politics": Sydney Ember and Maggie Astor, "How Huge Voter Turnout Eluded Bernie Sanders on Super Tuesday," *New York Times*, Mar. 4, 2020, updated Mar. 7, 2020 https://www.nytimes.com/2020/03/04/us/politics/bernie-sanders-young-voter-turnout.html?auth=login-email&login=email ;____. "Hey Kids: Get Out There and Vote!" *New York Times*, Apr. 12, 2020, E 12. https://www.nytimes.com/2020/04/12/opinion/biden-sanders-young-voters.html?searchResultPosition=1 .

IV. WILL YOU?

Why Vote?

2000 margin: Elving, "The Florida Recount of 2000."

2016 margin: Philip Bunt, "Trump will be president thanks to 80,000 people in three states," *Washington Post*, Dec. 1, 2016 https://www.washingtonpost.com/news/the-fix/wp/2016/12/01/donald-trump-will-be-president-thanks-to-80000-people-in-three-states/ .

Emerson, "Those who stay": Ralph Waldo Emerson, *The Journals and Miscellaneous Notebooks of Ralph Waldo Emerson, Volume XV 1*, Ed. by Linda Allardt, David W. Hill, and Ruth H. Bennett, 1982 (Cambridge, MA and London: Belknap Press, 1982), 205.

Harvard Kennedy School Institute of Politics. Harvard Youth Poll. 39th Edition, Spring 2020, Apr. 23, 2020 https://iop.harvard.edu/youth-poll/harvard-youth-poll .

John Quincy Adams, "Always vote": Nicandro Iannacci, "10 facts about John Quincy Adams on his birthday," July 11, 2018, Constitution Daily, National Constitution Center, https://constitutioncenter.org/blog/10-fascinating-facts-about-john-quincy-adams-for-his-248th-birthday .

Twain, "But in": "Mark Twain Talks On Graft. Says Voters Can Rise and Stamp It Out," Interview, Nov. 6, 1905, *Boston Transcript*, on twainquotes.com http://www.twainquotes.com/interviews/Interview6Nov1905.html

Eisenhower, "Our American": Dwight D. Eisenhower, ed. Allan Taylor, *What Eisenhower Thinks*, (New York: Thomas Y. Crowell Co., 1952), 48.

Roosevelt, "Nobody will": Radio Address from the White House, Oct. 5, 1944, *The Public Papers and Addresses of Franklin D. Roosevelt, 1944-45*, (New York: Harper & Brothers, 1950), 318, https://quod.lib.umich.edu/p/ppotpus/4926605.1944.001/396?page=root;rgn=works;size=100;view=image;q1=roosevelt%2C+franklin;op2=and;q2=American+people+of+the+right+to+vote.

Anthony, "Someone struggled": widely attributed. See https://www.msn.com/en-us/news/politics/women-are-proudly-covering-susan-b-anthony's-grave-in-"i-voted"-stickers/ar-BBPpLFK.

One More Thing

You're off to great places!"; "Oh, the places you'll go!": Dr. Seuss, *Oh, the Places You'll Go!* (New York: Random House, 1990), 1.

Victor, "No one should": Ashley Southall, "A 102-Year-Old Face of Voting Delays at the State of the Union," *New York Times*, Feb. 12, 2013, https://thecaucus.blogs.nytimes.com/2013/02/12/a-102-year-old-face-of-voting-delays-at-the-state-of-the-union/ .

Victor, "perpetuation of racial entitlement"; "Justice Scalia": Clare Kim, "Desilene Victor to Justice Scalia: 'Voting Rights Act is not a racial entitlement," NBC News.com, updated Mar. 18, 2013. http://www.nbcnews.com/id/51234068/t/desiline-victor-justice-scalia-voting-rights-act-not-racial-entitlement/#.XvqJES2ZOX1 .

Victor, "Vote" and hat reference: David Usborne, "Desilene Victor at 102 queued for six hours to vote for Obama. Now 106, she just early voted for Hillary Clinton," Independent, Nov. 7, 2016 https://www.independent.co.uk/news/world/americas/us-elections/desiline-victor-106-stood-in-line-barack-obama-hillary-clinton-miami-black-turnout-florida-a7401696.html .

Franklin, "A republic": Gillian Brockell, "'A republic, if you can keep it': Did Ben Franklin really say Impeachment Day's favorite quote?" *Washington Post*, Dec. 18, 2019 https://www.washingtonpost.com/history/2019/12/18/republic-if-you-can-keep-it-did-ben-franklin-really-say-impeachment-days-favorite-quote/.

"republic": Definition of "republic," *Merriam-Webster Dictionary* https://www.merriam-webster.com/dictionary/republic (accessed June 29, 2020).

Appendix E

"great cakes" and Hartford: Maia Surdam, "Election Cake," AHA Today, Nov. 1, 2016 https://www.historians.org/publications-and-directories/perspectives-on-history/november-2016/election-cake-a-forgotten-democratic-tradition (accessed Jun. 29, 2020); Linda Stradley, "Election Day Cake History and Recipe," https://whatscookingamerica.net/History/Cakes/ElectionCake.htm (accessed Jun. 29, 2020).

Simmons, Amelia. *American Cookery*. A Facsimile of the Second Edition Printed in Albany, 1796. Bedford, MA: Applewood Books, 1996.

Old World Levain Bakery" and "#makeamericacakeagain": Keia Mastrianni, "Election Cake" Makes a Modern Day Resurgence," *Bon Appetit*, Oct. 17, 2016 https://www.bonappetit.com/entertaining-style/trends-news/article/election-cake-history (accessed June 29, 2020).

BIBLIOGRAPHY

I. Legislative and Executive Documents

Administrator of General Services. "Certification of Amendment to Constitution of the United States Extending the Right to Vote to Citizens Eighteen Years of Age or Older." *Federal Register* 36, no. 130 (July 7, 1971) http://cdn.loc.gov/service/ll/fedreg/fr036/fr036130/fr036130.pdf.

National Commission on the Causes and Prevention of Violence. *To Establish Justice, to Insure Domestic Tranquility: Final Report of the National Commission on the Causes and Prevention of Violence.* Washington, DC: General Printing Office, Dec. 10, 1969.

Report of the Commission on Voting Participation and Registration. President Lyndon B. Johnson. Washington, DC. Dec.20, 1963.

U.S. Congress. *Congressional Record.* 1917-18, 1941–71, Washington, DC.

U.S. Congress. House. Committee on the Judiciary, Subcommittee No. 1. *A Joint Resolution Proposing an Amendment to the Constitution of the United States; Extending the Right to Vote to Citizens Eighteen Years of Age or Older.* 78th Cong., 1st sess., Oct. 20, 1943.

U.S. Congress. House. *For the People Act of 2019*, HR 1, 116th Cong., 1st sess., introduced in House Jan. 3, 2019 https://www.congress.gov/bill/116th-congress/house-bill/1.

U.S. Congress. Senate. Committee on the Judiciary, Subcommittee on Constitutional Amendments. *Proposing an Amendment to the Constitution of the United States to Grant to Citizens of the United States Who Have Attained the Age of Eighteen the Right to Vote.* 82d Cong., 2d sess., June 27, 1952.

U.S. Congress. Senate. Committee on the Judiciary, Subcommittee on Constitutional Amendments. *Proposing an Amendment to the Constitution of the United States to Grant to Citizens of the United States Who Have Attained the Age of Eighteen the Right to Vote.* 83rd Cong., 1st sess., June 2, July 13, 1953.

U.S. Congress. Senate. Committee on the Judiciary. *Proposing an Amendment to the Constitution of the United States to Grant to Citizens of the United States Who Have Attained the Age of 18 the Right to Vote.* 83rd Cong., 2d sess., Mar. 1, 1954.

U.S. Congress. Senate. Committee on the Judiciary. *Interim Report: Comic Books and Juvenile Delinquency.* 83rd Cong., 1- 2d sess., Mar. 14, 1955.

U.S. Congress. Senate. Committee on the Judiciary. Subcommittee on Constitutional Amendments. *Hearings Before the Subcommittee on Constitutional Amendments on the Committee of the Judiciary United States Senate Eighty-Seventh Congress First Session on S.J. Res. 1, S.J. Res. 2, S.J. Res. 4, S.J. Res. 9, S.J. Res. 12, S.J. Res. 16, S.J. Res. 23, S.J. Res. 26, S.J. Res. 28, S.J. Res. 48, S.J. Res. 96, S.J. Res. 1-2, S.J. Res. 113, and S.J. Res. 114,*

Proposing Amendments to the Constitution Relating to the Method of Nomination and Election of the President and Vice President and S.J. Res. 14, S.J. Res. 20, S.J. Res. 54, S.J. Res. 58, S.J. Res. 67, S.J. Res. 71, S.J. Res. 81, and S.J. Res. 90, Proposing Amendment to the Constitution Relating to Qualifications for Voting. 87th Cong., 1st sess., May 23, 26, June 8, 27–29, July 13, 1961.

U.S. Congress. Senate. Committee on the Judiciary. Subcommittee on Constitutional Amendments. *Hearings Before the Subcommittee on Constitutional Amendments of the Committee of the Judiciary United States Senate Ninetieth Congress Second Session on S.J. Res. 8, S.J. Res. 14, and S.J. Res. 78 Relating to Lowering the Voting Age to 18.* 90th Cong., 2d sess., May 14–16, 1968.

U.S. Congress. Senate. Committee on the Judiciary. Subcommittee on Constitutional Amendments. *Hearings Before the Subcommittee on Constitutional Amendments of the Committee of the Judiciary United States Senate Ninety-First Congress Second Session on S.J. Res. 7, S.J. Res. 19, S.J. Res. 32, S.J. Res. 34, S.J. Res. 38, S.J. Res. 73, S.J. Res. 73, S.J. Res. 87, S.J. Res. 102, S.J. Res. 105, S.J. Res. 141, S.J. Res. 147.* 91st Cong., 2d sess., Feb. 16–17, Mar. 9–10, 1970.

U.S. Congress. Senate. Committee on the Judiciary. Subcommittee on Constitutional Amendments. Committee Print: *Lowering the Voting Age to 18: A Fifty State Survey of the Costs and Other Problems of Dual-Age Voting.* 92d Cong., 1st sess., Feb. 1971.

U.S. Congress. Senate. Committee on the Judiciary. Subcommittee on Constitutional Amendments. Committee Print: *Passage and Ratification of the Twenty-sixth Amendment.* 92d Cong., 1st sess., Sept. 1971.

II. Judicial Documents

Constitution of the United States.

Brown v. Board of Ed., 347 US 483 (1954).

Bush v. Gore, 531 U.S. 98 (2000).

Dred Scott v. Sandford, 60 U.S. 393 (1857).

Katzenbach v. Morgan, 384 U.S. 641 (1966).

Oregon v. Mitchell, 400 U.S. 112 (1970).

Shelby County v. Holder, 570 U.S. 529 (2103).

III. Interviews, Letters, Oral Histories, Reflections, Remarks, and Speeches

Adams, Abigail. Abigail Adams to John Adams, 31 Mar. - 5 Apr. 1776 [electronic edition]. Adams Family Papers: An Electronic Archive. Massachusetts Historical Society. http://www.masshist.org/digitaladams/

Adams, John. John Adams to James Sullivan, 26 May 1776. In Founders Online, National Archives, version of Jan. 18, 2019, https://founders.archives.gov/documents/

Adams/06-04-02-0091. [Original source: The Adams Papers, Papers of John Adams, vol. 4, February–August 1776, ed. Robert J. Taylor. Cambridge, MA: Harvard University Press, 1979].

Anthony, Susan B. "Is it a Crime for a U.S. Citizen to Vote? Speech, ____, Apr. 3, 1873." Voices of Democracy: The U.S. Oratory Project. https://voicesofdemocracy. umd.edu/anthony-is-it-a-crime-speech-text/ [citing Gordon, Ann D., ed. *The Selected Papers of Elizabeth Cady Stanton and Susan B. Anthony, Volume II: An Aristocracy of Sex, 1866-1873.* Copyright 2000 by Rutgers, the State University of New Jersey. Reprinted by permission of Rutgers University Press.]

Boren, Lyle. "Congressional speech given by Lyle Boren on the floor." Remarks, Washington, D.C., Jan. 10, 1940. John Steinbeck's America, accessed Feb. 28, 2020, http:// steinbeck.oucreate.com/items/show/34.

Bickel, Alexander, Charles Black, Jr., Robert Bork, John Hart Ely, Louis Pollak, & Eugene Rostow. Letter to the Editor, Amendment Favored for Lowering Voting Age. *New York Times*, Apr. 5, 1970. https://timesmachine.nytimes.com/timesma-chine/1970/04/05/354797882.html?pageNumber=171 .

Cox, Archibald and Paul Freund. Letter to the Editor, Power of Congress to Lower Voting Age Upheld. *New York Times*, Apr. 12, 1970. https://timesmachine.nytimes. com/timesmachine/1970/04/12/121522975.html?pageNumber=172 .

de Tocqueville, Alexis D., (Henry Reeve, transl.) *Democracy in America* (Chapter IV: The Principle Of The Sovereignty Of The People In America). Project Gutenberg, last updated 2013, https://www.gutenberg.org/files/815/815-h/815-h.ht-m#link2HCH0008.

de Tocqueville, Alexis, *Letters from America* (trans. By Frederick Brown) (Letter from de Tocqueville to his mother, May 14, 1831). New Haven: Yale University Press, 2010 in https://hudsonreview.com/2013/03/letters-from-america/#.XqCGTS2ZP1I.

Douglass, Frederick B. "What the Black Man Wants." Speech, Boston, MA , April 1865. Ashbrook Center at Ashland University. https://teachingamericanhistory.org/ library/document/what-the-black-man-wants/

Douglass, Frederick B. "Why Should a Colored Man Enlist? " Speech, Boston, MA , April 1863. Ashbrook Center at Ashland University. https://teachingamericanhistory. org/library/document/why-should-a-colored-man-enlist/.

Eisenhower, Dwight D. "Annual Message to the Congress on the State of the Union. January 7, 1954." Online by Gerhard Peters and John T. Woolley, The American Presidency Project. https://www.presidency.ucsb.edu/node/232936.

Eisenhower, Dwight D. and ed. Allan Taylor. *What Eisenhower Thinks*, New York: Thomas Y. Crowell Co., 1952.

Fredericks, Gloria. "Remarks to the Delegates of the Alaska Constitutional Convention. January 13, 1956." University of Alaska, "Creating Alaska - The Origins of the 49th State." https://www.alaska.edu/creatingalaska/constitutional-convention/speeches-to-the-conventio/speeches-to-the-conventio/fredericks/.

Hamilton, Alexander. *The Farmer Refuted, or A more impartial and comprehensive View of the Dispute between Great-Britain and the Colonies. . . ..*New York, 1775, in Syrett, Harold C., ed., *The Papers of Alexander Hamilton.* New York: Columbia University Press, 1961-1979 https://www.dhr.history.vt.edu/modules/us/mod03_rev/evidence_detail_13.html.

Kennedy, Edward M. Interview by James Sterling Young, April 3, 2007. Edward M. Kennedy Oral History Project, Miller Center, University of Virginia. https://millercenter.org/the-presidency/presidential-oral-histories/edward-m-kennedy-oral-history-432007.

Kennedy, John F. "Inaugural Address. January 20, 1961." Online by Gerhard Peters and John T. Woolley, The American Presidency Project. https://www.presidency.ucsb.edu/node/234470.

King, Martin Luther, Jr. "Beyond Vietnam." Speech, New York, NY., April 4, 1967. The Martin Luther King, Jr. Research and Education Institute, Stanford University. https://kinginstitute.stanford.edu/king-papers/documents/beyond-vietnam.

King, Martin Luther, Jr. "Give Us The Ballot." Speech, Washington, DC, May 17, 1957. The Martin Luther King, Jr. Research and Education Institute, Stanford University. https://kinginstitute.stanford.edu/king-papers/documents/give-us-ballot-address-delivered-prayer-pilgrimage-freedom.

King, Jr. Martin Luther. "I Have A Dream…" Speech, March on Washington, DC, Aug. 28, 1963. U.S. National Archives and Records Administration. https://www.archives.gov/files/press/exhibits/dream-speech.pdf

Johnson, Lyndon B. "President Johnson's Special Message to the Congress: The American Promise. March 15, 1965." In *Public Papers of the Presidents of the United States: Lyndon B. Johnson, 1965, Volume I.* Washington, DC: Government Printing Office, 1966.

Johnson, Lyndon B. "Remarks on the Signing of the Voting Rights Act. August 6, 1965." Miller Center of Public Affairs, University of Virginia. https://millercenter.org/the-presidency/presidential-speeches/august-6-1965-remarks-signing-voting-rights-act.

Lewis, John. "An Oral History of Selma and the Struggle for the Voting Rights Act," December 25, 2014, *Time,* https://time.com/3647070/selma-john-lewis-voting-rights-act/.

Malcolm X. "The Ballot or the Bullet." Speech, King Solomon Baptist Church, Detroit, Michigan, April 12, 1964. American Public Media. http://americanradioworks.publicradio.org/features/blackspeech/mx.html.

McHenry, James. Diary, September 18, 1787. Manuscript. James McHenry Papers, Manuscript Division, Library of Congress (63.02.00) [Digital ID# us0063_02p1]. In Bell, Dana, "A Republic, If You Can Keep It." https://blogs.loc.gov/teachers/2016/09/a-republic-if-you-can-keep-it/.

Nixon, Richard. "Remarks at a Ceremony Marking the Certification of the 26th Amendment to the Constitution. July 5, 1971." Online by Gerhard Peters and John T. Woolley, The American Presidency Project. https://www.presidency.ucsb.edu/node/240368.

Nixon, Richard. "Statement About Ratification of the 26th Amendment to the Constitution. June 30, 1971." Online by Gerhard Peters and John T. Woolley, The American Presidency Project. https://www.presidency.ucsb.edu/node/240351.

Nixon, Richard. "Statement of Signing the Voting Rights Act Amendments of 1970. June 22, 1970." Public Papers of the Presidents of the United States: Richard M. Nixon, 1970. Washington DC: Government Printing Office, 1971.

Parker, Carey. Interview by James Sterling Young, September, 22, 2008, Edward M. Kennedy Oral History Project, Miller Center, University of Virginia. https://www.emkinstitute.org/resources/carey-parker-09-2008.

Ramsey, William. "26th Amendment Certification." "Personal Reflection of the Certification." Phyllis and Bill Ramsey Web Site: A Retrospect of Half a Century, 2012. http://drwmramsey.com/amendment.html.

Roosevelt, Eleanor. "My Day, January 21, 1943," The Eleanor Roosevelt Papers Digital Edition (2017), accessed 2/28/2019, https://www2.gwu.edu/~erpapers/myday/displaydocedits.cfm?_y=1943&_f=md056400.

Roosevelt, Franklin D. "Fireside Chat 23. October 12, 1942." Online by Gerhard Peters and John T. Woolley, The American Presidency Project. https://www.presidency.ucsb.edu/node/209991.

Roosevelt, Franklin D. "Fireside Chat 23: On the Home Front. October 12, 1942." Miller Center, University of Virginia. https://millercenter.org/the-presidency/presidential-speeches/october-12-1942-fireside-chat-23-home-front.

Roosevelt, Franklin D. "Statement on Peace Time Universal Selective Service. September 16, 1940." Online by Gerhard Peters and John T. Woolley, The American Presidency Project. https://www.presidency.ucsb.edu/node/210454.

Wilson, Woodrow. "Equal Suffrage." Address of the President of the United States. U.S. Senate. September 30, 1918. Washington, DC: Government Printing Office: 1918. https://www.senate.gov/artandhistory/history/resources/pdf/WilsonSpeech1918.pdf.

"1994 White House Correspondents' Dinner," C-SPAN, Apr. 23, 1994 https://www.c-span.org/video/?56320-1/1994-white-house-correspondents-dinner .

IV. Data, Polls, and Research

____. "2014 Youth Turnout and Registration Rates Lowest Ever Recorded." Center for Information & Research on Civic Learning and Engagement, July 21, 2015.https://circle.tufts.edu/latest-research/2014-youth-turnout-and-registration-rates-lowest-ever-recorded.

____. "2016 Election Center." Center for Information & Research on Civic Learning and Engagement. https://circle.tufts.edu/2016-election-center.

____. "2018 Election Center." Center for Information & Research on Civic Learning and Engagement. https://circle.tufts.edu/2018-election-center#exclusive-circle-polling.

____. "2018 Youth Voter Turnout Increased In Every State." Center for Information & Research on Civic Learning and Engagement, Apr. 2, 2019. https://circle.tufts.edu/latest-research/2018-youth-voter-turnout-increased-every-state?utm_source=Tisch+College+Contact+List&utm_campaign=263675b880-EMAIL_CAMPAIGN_2019_04_29_08_27&utm_medium=email&utm_term=0_246da4d028-263675b880-144249329.

____. "Election Night 2016: 24 Million Youth Voted, Most Rejected Trump." Center for Information & Research on Civic Learning and Engagement, Nov. 14, 2016. https://circle.tufts.edu/latest-research/election-night-2016-24-million-youth-voted-most-rejected-trump.

____. "Election Night 2018: Historically High Youth Turnout, Support for Democrats." Center for Information & Research on Civic Learning and Engagement, Nov. 7, 2018. https://circle.tufts.edu/latest-research/election-night-2018-historically-high-youth-turnout-support-democrats.

____. "Five Takeaways on Social Media and the Youth Vote in 2018." Center for Information & Research on Civic Learning and Engagement, Nov. 15, 2018. https://circle.tufts.edu/latest-research/five-takeaways-social-media-and-youth-vote-2018.

____. "How Obama Won Re-election." *New York Times*, updated Nov. 7, 2012. https://archive.nytimes.com/www.nytimes.com/interactive/2012/11/07/us/politics/obamas-diverse-base-of-support.html?searchResultPosition=3.

____. "So Much for "Slacktivism": Youth Translate Online Engagement to Offline Political Action." Center for Information & Research on Civic Learning and Engagement, Oct. 15, 2018. https://circle.tufts.edu/latest-research/so-much-slacktivism-youth-translate-online-engagement-offline-political-action.

____. "Voter Enthusiasm at Record High in Nationalized Midterm Environment." Pew Research Center, Sept. 26, 2018. https://www.people-press.org/2018/09/26/voter-enthusiasm-at-record-high-in-nationalized-midterm-environment/.

____. "Voting and Registration in the Election of November 2006," U.S. Census Bureau, June 2008, https://www.census.gov/prod/2008pubs/p20-557.pdf .

____. "Voting Rates by Age." U.S. Census Bureau, May 10, 2017.https://www.census.gov/library/visualizations/2017/comm/voting-rates-age.html.

____. "Young People More Engaged, More Uncertain." Pew Research Center, Sept. 30, 2004 https://www.people-press.org/2004/09/30/young-people-more-engaged-more-uncertain/.

____. "Young Voters Supported Obama Less, But May Have Mattered More." Pew Research Center, Nov. 26, 2012. https://www.pewresearch.org/politics/2012/11/26/young-voters-supported-obama-less-but-may-have-mattered-more/ .

____. "Youth Engagement Falls; Registration Also Declines." Sept. 28, 2012. Pew Research Center. https://www.people-press.org/2012/09/28/youth-engagement-falls-registration-also-declines/.

____. "Youth in the Age of Obama." *New York Times*, Oct. 2, 2013. https://archive.nytimes.com/www.nytimes.com/interactive/2013/02/10/us/0210-democrats-winning-the-young-voters.html?searchResultPosition=5.

Brewer, F. "The Voting Age." Editorial research reports 1944 (Vol. II). Washington, DC: CQ Press, 1944. https://library.cqpress.com/cqresearcher/document.php?id=cqresrre1944090900.

Carroll, Joseph. "How Many Are Planning to Vote for the First Time?" Gallup News Service, Oct. 25, 2004. https://news.gallup.com/poll/13744/how-many-planning-vote-first-time.aspx.

Cilluffo, Anthony and Fry, Richard. "An early look at the 2020 electorate." January 30, 2019. Pew Research Center. https://www.pewsocialtrends.org/essay/an-early-look-at-the-2020-electorate/.

Colby, Sandra L. and Jennifer M. Ortman. "The Baby Boom Cohort in the United States: 2012 to 2060." May 2014. U.S. Census Bureau. https://www.census.gov/prod/2014pubs/p25-1141.pdf.

Dickinson Jr., W. B. "Voting in 1960." Editorial research reports 1960 (Vol. II). Washington, DC: CQ Press, 1960. Retrieved from http://library.cqpress.com/cqresearcher/cqresrre1960092100.

File, Thom. "Voting in America: A Look at the 2016 Presidential Election." May 10, 2017, U.S. Census Bureau. https://www.census.gov/newsroom/blogs/random-samplings/2017/05/voting_in_america.html.

File, Thom. "Voting in America: A Look at the 2016 Presidential Election." May 10, 2017, U.S. Census Bureau.

https://www.census.gov/content/dam/Census/library/publications/2015/demo/p20-577.pdf .

File, Thom. "Young-Adult Voting: An Analysis of Presidential Elections, 1964–2012." Current Population Survey Reports. Washington DC: U.S. Census Bureau, 2013. https://www.census.gov/prod/2014pubs/p20-573.pdf.

Harvard Kennedy School Institute of Politics. Harvard Youth Poll. 39th Edition, Spring 2020, Apr. 23, 2020 https://iop.harvard.edu/youth-poll/harvard-youth-poll .

Lyons, Linda. "Gallup Brain: History of the Youth Vote." Gallup. Jan. 20, 2004. https://news.gallup.com/poll/10348/gallup-brain-history-youth-vote.aspx.

Neale, Thomas H. "The Eighteen Year Old Vote: The Twenty-Sixth Amendment and Subsequent Voting Rates of Newly Enfranchised Age Groups." DC: Congressional Research Service, 1983. https://www.everycrsreport.com/files/19830520_83-103GOV_f7c90f8fb698968e03f7ce5e3b45288dffcce08f.pdf

Packman, M. "Eighteen-year-old and soldier voting." Editorial research reports 1954 (Vol. I). Washington, DC: CQ Press, 1954. Retrieved from http://library.cqpress.com/cqresearcher/cqresrre1954022400.

Rainie, Lee. "Internet Election News Audience Seeks Convenience, Familiar Names," Dec. 3, 2000. Pew Research Center. https://www.pewresearch.org/internet/2000/12/03/internet-election-news-audience-seeks-convenience-familiar-names/.

Report of the Commission on Youth Voting and Civic Knowledge. "All Together Now: Collaboration and Innovation for Youth Engagement." (Medford, MA: Center for Information & Research on Civic Learning and Engagement, 2013). https://circle.tufts.edu/our-research/broadening-youth-voting/commission-youth-voting-and-civic-knowledge .

Rosentiel, Tom and Scott Keeter. "Cell-Only Voters Not Very Different." Oct. 26, 2006. Pew Research Center. https://www.pewresearch.org/2006/10/26/cellonly-voters-not-very-different/.

Rosentiel, Tom and Scott Keeter. "Election '06: Big Changes in Some Key Groups." Nov. 16, 2006. Pew Research Center. https://www.pewresearch.org/2006/11/16/election-06-big-changes-in-some-key-groups/.

Rosentiel, Tom, Scott Keeter, Juliana Horowitz, Alec Tyson. "Young Voters in the 2008 Election." Nov. 13, 2008, Pew Research Center. https://www.pewresearch.org/2008/11/13/young-voters-in-the-2008-election/.

Silver, Nate and Dhrumil Mehta. "Both Republicans And Democrats Have an Age Problem." Apr. 28, 2014. FiveThirtyEight. https://fivethirtyeight.com/features/both-republicans-and-democrats-have-an-age-problem/.

Thomas, N., Bergom, I., Casellas Connors, I., Gautam, P., Gismondi, A., & Roshko, A. (2017). "Democracy counts: A report on U.S. college and university student voting." 2017. Institute for Democracy & Higher Education, Tufts University's Jonathan M. Tisch College of Civic Life. https://idhe.tufts.edu/sites/default/files/NSLVE%20Report%202012-2016-092117%5B3%5D.pdf.

U.S. Census Bureau. Current Population Reports. Series P-20, No. 322. "Voting and Registration in the Election of November 1976." U.S. Government Printing Office, Washington, D.C., 1978. https://www.census.gov/content/dam/Census/library/publications/1978/demo/p20-322.pdf.

U.S. Census Bureau. "Historical Reported Voting Rates." Last Revised Oct. 7, 2019. https://www.census.gov/data/tables/time-series/demo/voting-and-registration/voting-historical-time-series.html.

U.S. Census Bureau. "Reported Voting Rates in Presidential Election Years by Selected Characteristics: Nov. 1964 to 2016." https://www.census.gov/data/tables/time-series/demo/voting-and-registration/voting-historical-time-series.html.

U.S. Census Bureau. "Voting Rates by Age." May 10, 2017. https://www.census.gov/library/visualizations/2017/comm/voting-rates-age.html.

V. Articles

____."18-Year-Old Vote." In CQ Almanac 1954, 10th ed., 08-417. Washington, DC: Congressional Quarterly, 1955. http://library.cqpress.com/cqalmanac/cqal54-1359412.

____."18-Year-Old Vote: Constitutional Amendment Cleared." In CQ Almanac 1971, 27th ed., 05-475-05-477. Washington, DC: Congressional Quarterly, 1972. http://library.cqpress.com/cqalmanac/cqal71-1253597.

____. "Ben Franklin's Two Birthdays." The Franklin Institute, https://www.fi.edu/benjamin-franklin/happy-birthday-ben-franklin (accessed Jun. 30, 2020).

____."Congress Lowers Voting Age, Extends Voting Rights Act." In CQ Almanac 1970, 26th ed., 05-192-05-199. Washington, DC: Congressional Quarterly, 1971. http://library.cqpress.com/cqalmanac/cqal70-1292888.

____. "Harnessing the Youth Tide." New York Times, June 30, 1968, E 12. https://timesmachine.nytimes.com/timesmachine/1968/06/30/79941377.html?pageNumber=147.

____. "Hey Kids: Get Out There and Vote!" New York Times, Apr. 12, 2020, E 12. https://timesmachine.nytimes.com/timesmachine/1968/06/30/79941377.html?pageNumber=147. https://www.nytimes.com/2020/04/12/opinion/biden-sanders-young-voters.html?searchResultPosition=1 .

____. "The Golden Age of MTV - And Yes, There Was One." NPR. Heard on All Things Considered. Nov. 6, 2011. https://www.npr.org/2011/11/06/141991877/the-golden-age-of-mtv-and-yes-there-was-one [Rob Tannenbaum, Laura Sullivan interview]

____. "The Youth Vote." New York Times, Aug. 21, 1972, 30. https://timesmachine.nytimes.com/timesmachine/1972/08/21/81956818.html?pageNumber=30.

____. "Who We Are." NextGen America, https://nextgenamerica.org/about-us/ (accessed Jun. 30, 2020).

99% Invisible and Whitney Jones. "Why R.E.M.'s Out of Time Is the Most Politically Significant Album in U.S. History," Slate, July 25, 2014. http://www.slate.com/blogs/the_eye/2014/07/25/roman_mars_99_percent_invisible_r_e_m_s_out_of_time_is_the_most_politically.html.

Adler, Renata. "Going 'Wild in the Streets." New York Times, June 16, 1968, D1. https://timesmachine.nytimes.com/timesmachine/1968/06/16/91230230.html?pageNumber=117.

Alcindor, Yamiche. "Hillary Clinton Gains Some Ground Among Young Voters, Poll Finds." New York Times, Oct. 26, 2016. https://www.nytimes.com/2016/10/27/us/politics/hillary-clinton-gains-some-ground-among-young-voters-poll-finds.html?searchResultPosition=45.

Apple, Jr., R. W. "The States Ratify Full Vote at 18." New York Times, July 1, 1971, 1. https://timesmachine.nytimes.com/timesmachine/1971/07/01/79672237.html?pageNumber=1 .

Associated Press. "54% Voted in '76 Election," *New York Times*, Apr. 16, 1976, 30. https://timesmachine.nytimes.com/timesmachine/1978/04/16/139844872.html?pageNumber=30.

Associated Press. "Plans to Lower Voting Age Defeated in Most States." *New York Times*, Nov. 5, 1970, 38. https://timesmachine.nytimes.com/timesmachine/1970/11/05/129428682.html?pageNumber=38 .

Associated Press. "Reagan Makes Bid for Youths' Votes." *New York Times*, Oct. 28, 1984, 28. https://timesmachine.nytimes.com/timesmachine/1984/10/28/041931.html?pageNumber=28.

Badger, Emily and Claire Cain Miller. "How the Trump Era Is Molding the Next Generation of Voter." *New York Times*, Apr. 1, 2019. https://www.nytimes.com/2019/04/01/upshot/trump-era-molding-young-voters.html?action=click&module=RelatedCoverage&pgtype=Article&region=Footer.

Bauer-Wolf, Jeremy. "Knocking Down Barriers for Student Voting." *Inside Higher Ed*, Mar. 20, 2019. https://www.insidehighered.com/news/2019/03/20/house-democrats-election-bill-makes-it-easier-college-students-vote-experts-say .

Bauer-Wolf, Jeremy. "Optimism for Student Vote Turnout." *Inside Higher Ed*, Aug. 14, 2018. https://www.insidehighered.com/news/2018/08/14/advocacy-groups-expect-uptick-college-student-voter-turnout .

Bellis, Mary. "The History of Mr. Potato Head." ThoughtCo., updated Jan. 19, 2019 https://www.thoughtco.com/history-of-mr-potato-head-1992311.

Brockell, Gillian. "'A republic, if you can keep it': Did Ben Franklin really say Impeachment Day's favorite quote?" *Washington Post*, Dec. 18, 2019 https://www.washingtonpost.com/history/2019/12/18/republic-if-you-can-keep-it-did-ben-franklin-really-say-impeachment-days-favorite-quote/

Bunt, Philip. "Trump will be president thanks to 80,000 people in three states." *Washington Post*, Dec. 1, 2016. https://www.washingtonpost.com/news/the-fix/wp/2016/12/01/donald-trump-will-be-president-thanks-to-80000-people-in-three-states/ .

Butler, Bethonie. "President Obama tells 'spooky story' to Samantha Bee: 'Donald Trumo could be president.'" *Washington Post*, Nov. 1, 2016https://www.washingtonpost.com/news/arts-and-entertainment/wp/2016/11/01/president-obama-tells-spooky-story-to-samantha-bee-donald-trump-could-be-president/.

Calmes, Jackie. "Obama Courts the Votes of a Less-Engaged Youth." *New York Times*, Aug. 28, 2012. https://www.nytimes.com/2012/08/29/us/politics/obama-heads-to-campus-to-press-for-young-voters.html?searchResultPosition=2.

Chen, David W. "In Nader Supporters' Math, Gore Equals Bush." *New York Times*, Oct. 15, 2000, 28. https://timesmachine.nytimes.com/timesmachine/2000/10/15/672351.html?pageNumber=27 .

Corbyn, Zoe. "Facebook experiment boosts US voter turnout." Sept. 12, 2012, nature https://www.nature.com/news/facebook-experiment-boosts-us-voter-turnout-1.11401.

Couch, Robbie."87% Of Millennials Donated To Charity Last Year And You Should Stop Calling Them Selfish: Report." HuffPost, updated Dec. 6, 2017. https://www.huffpost.com/entry/millennials-volunteer-charity-giving_n_5507778.

Della Volpe, John. "The young don't vote? This time they will. And school shootings are the difference." *Washington Post*, Oct. 29, 2018. https://www.washingtonpost.com/outlook/2018/10/29/young-dont-vote-this-time-they-will-school-shootings-are-difference/?noredirect=on.

Dewan, Shaila K. "Youths Use Varied Strategies to Feel Their way to Choices." Oct. 30, 2000, *New York Times*, 17. https://timesmachine.nytimes.com/timesmachine/2000/10/30/924059.html?pageNumber=16 .

de Witt, Karen. "MTV Puts the Campaign on Fast Forward." *New York Times*, Feb. 8, 1992, 8. https://www.nytimes.com/1992/02/08/us/the-1992-campaign-media-mtv-puts-the-campaign-on-fast-forward.html?searchResultPosition=29.

Dionne, Jr., E. J. "G.O.P. Makes Reagan Lure Of Young a Long-Term Asset." *New York Times*. Oct. 31, 1988, 1. https://www.nytimes.com/1988/10/31/us/political-memo-gop-makes-reagan-lure-of-young-a-long-term-asset.html?searchResultPosition=12.

D.K. "Why young people don't vote." *The Economist*, Oct. 29, 2014. https://www.economist.com/the-economist-explains/2014/10/29/why-young-people-dont-vote.

Ditzian, Eric. "Bill Clinton to Barack Obama: MTV's History With Politics." MTV News, Oct. 12, 2010. http://www.mtv.com/news/1649854/bill-clinton-to-barack-obama-mtvs-history-with-politics/.

Dowd, Maureen. "Mondale, Pursuing Student Vote, Accuses Reagan of 'Absurdity'". *New York Times*, Apr. 8, 1984, 36. https://timesmachine.nytimes.com/timesmachine/1984/04/08/109063.html?pageNumber=36.

Dowd, Maureen. "Why Are All the Politicians Watching Rock Video?" New York Times, Apr. 19, 1985, 18 https://timesmachine.nytimes.com/timesmachine/1985/04/19/178774.html?pageNumber=18.

Eaton, Anne T. "Books for Children." *New York Times*, Feb. 12, 1933. https://timesmachine.nytimes.com/timesmachine/1933/02/12/issue.html

Egan, Timothy. "Vote Drives Gain Avid Attention of Youth in '04." *New York Times*, Sept. 15, 2004. https://www.nytimes.com/2004/09/15/politics/campaign/vote-drives-gain-avid-attention-of-youth-in-04.html?searchResultPosition=1 .

Ember, Sydney and Maggie Astor, "How Huge Voter Turnout Eluded Bernie Sanders on Super Tuesday." *New York Times*, Mar. 4, 2020, updated Mar. 7, 2020 https://www.nytimes.com/2020/03/04/us/politics/bernie-sanders-young-voter-turnout.html?auth=login-email&login=email

Epstein, Kayla and Emily Guskin. "Taylor Swift and Rihanna told young people to register. They're doing it, but are they going to actually vote?" *Washington Post*, Oct. 12, 2018 https://www.washingtonpost.com/politics/2018/10/12/taylor-swift-rihanna-told-young-people-register-theyre-doing-it-are-they-going-actually-vote/?noredirect=on.

Flegenheimer, Matt. "Hillary Clinton Tells College Students, 'I Need You.'" *New York Times*, Sept. 19, 2016. https://www.nytimes.com/2016/09/20/us/politics/hillary-clinton-speech-millennials.html?searchResultPosition=25.

Elving, Ron. "The Florida Recount of 2000: A Nightmare That Goes on Haunting," NPR. Nov. 12, 2018.
https://www.npr.org/2018/11/12/666812854/the-florida-recount-of-2000-a-nightmare-that-goes-on-haunting.

Ember, Sydney. "Young Voters Could Make a Difference. Will They?" *New York Times*, Nov. 2, 2018. https://www.nytimes.com/2018/11/02/us/politics/young-voters-midterms.html.

Flegenheimer, Matt. "Old Foes Bernie Sanders and Hillary Clinton Team Up to Woo the Kids." *New York Times*, Sept. 28, 2016. https://www.nytimes.com/2016/09/29/us/politics/bernie-sanders-hillary-clinton.html?searchResultPosition=27.

Frankel, Max. "President Won 49 States and 521 Electoral Votes." *New York Times*, Nov. 9, 1972, 1. https://timesmachine.nytimes.com/timesmachine/1972/11/09/79478407.html?pageNumber=25.

Freedberg, Louis. "Civics Problem: How to Get the Young to Vote." *New York Times*, Nov. 9, 1988, B10. https://www.nytimes.com/1988/11/09/us/education-civics-problem-how-to-get-the-young-to-vote.html?searchResultPosition=2.

Galston, William. A. and Clara Hendrickson. "How Millennials voted this election." Brookings Institute, Nov. 21, 2016.. https://www.brookings.edu/blog/fixgov/2016/11/21/how-millennials-voted/.

Graham, Fred P. "Again the Issue of the Voting Age." *New York Times*, May 19, 1968, 10E. https://timesmachine.nytimes.com/timesmachine/1968/05/19/88951031.html?pageNumber=219&auth=login-email.

Hahn, Rob. "50 years later, lessons we should learn from Gene McCarhy's 1968 campaign." Minneapolis Post, Mar. 16, 2018, https://www.minnpost.com/community-voices/2018/03/50-years-later-lessons-we-should-learn-gene-mccarthys-1968-campaign/.

Hitt, Jack. "What Ever Happened to Turtle Soup?" *Saveur*, Oct. 14, 2015. https://www.saveur.com/history-of-turtle-soup-hunting/.

Hoberman, J. "Are You Over 35? 'Wild in the Streets' Should Scare You." *New York Times*, Sept. 30, 2016. https://www.nytimes.com/2016/10/02/movies/wild-in-the-streets.html?searchResultPosition=1

Hunter, Marjorie. "400-to-19 Vote Finishes Action in Congress on Lowering of Age." *New York Times*, Mar. 2, 1971, 1. https://timesmachine.nytimes.com/timesmachine/1971/03/24/91275490.html?pageNumber=1 .

Ifill, Gwen. "Clinton Goes Eye to Eye with MTV Generation." *New York Times,* June 17, 1992, 22. https://www.nytimes.com/1992/06/17/us/the-1992-campaign-youth-vote-clinton-goes-eye-to-eye-with-mtv-generation.html?searchResultPosition=1.

Inman, William James. "Here's Why Young Voter Participation Is On The Rise." Newsy, Apr. 12, 2019. https://www.newsy.com/stories/young-voter-turnout-up-in-majority-of-states/?utm_source=Tisch+College+Contact+List&utm_campaign=263675b880-EMAIL_CAMPAIGN_2019_04_29_08_27&utm_medium=email&utm_term=0_246da4d028-263675b880-144249329.

Kaufman, Michael T. "First-Time Yale Voters Show Little Exuberance." *New York Times,* Nov. 7, 1972, 33. https://timesmachine.nytimes.com/timesmachine/1972/11/08/82230492.html?pageNumber=33.

Khadaroo, Stacy Teicher. "College-age voters: increasingly courted-and thwarted." Christian Science Monitor, Sept. 25, 2018. https://www.csmonitor.com/USA/Politics/2018/0925/College-age-voters-increasingly-courted-and-thwarted.

Khalid, Asma, Don Gonyea and Leila Fadel. "On The Sidelines Of Democracy: Exploring Why So Many Americans Don't Vote." Sept. 10, 2018, Morning Edition, NPR. https://www.npr.org/2018/09/10/645223716/on-the-sidelines-of-democracy-exploring-why-so-many-americans-dont-vote.

Kim, Clare. "Desilene Victor to Justice Scalia: 'Voting Rights Act is not a racial entitlement." NBC News.com, updated Mar. 18, 2013. http://www.nbcnews.com/id/51234068/t/desiline-victor-justice-scalia-voting-rights-act-not-racial-entitlement/#.XvqJES2ZOX1 .

King, Wayne. "Vote-at-18 Amendment Nearing Final Approval." *New York Times,* June 28, 1971, 35. https://timesmachine.nytimes.com/timesmachine/1971/06/28/79671949.html?pageNumber=35 .

King, Wayne and Warren Weaver, Jr. "Briefing: Seeking Youth." *New York Times,* May 19, 1986, 14. https://timesmachine.nytimes.com/timesmachine/1986/05/19/031286.html?pageNumber=14.

Klein, Christopher. "The Last Hours of the Nixon Presidency," Updated August 30, 2018, History.com https://www.history.com/news/the-last-hours-of-the-nixon-presidency-40-years-ago (accessed Mar. 3, 2020).

Kuekes, Edward. "Aftermath." *Cleveland Plain Dealer,* Nov. 9, 1952.

Lai, K.K. Rebecca and Allison McCann. "Exit Polls: How Voting Blocs Have Shifted From the '80s to Now." *New York Times,* Nov. 7, 2018. https://www.nytimes.com/interactive/2018/11/07/us/elections/house-exit-polls-analysis.html.

Lau, Tim. "The Rise in Midterm Voter Turnout Was Monumental." Nov. 9, 2018. Brennan Center for Justice. https://www.brennancenter.org/our-work/analysis-opinion/rise-midterm-voter-turnout-was-monumental.

Lawrence, Jill, "Bush, Perot Appear in Taped Interviews on MTV." *AP News,* Nov. 1, 1992. https://apnews.com/0c5067773012e145e5116e235eef9c30.

Lewis, Anthony. "And Now the Election." *New York Times*, July 19, 1976, 15 https://timesmachine.nytimes.com/timesmachine/1976/07/19/75634073.html?pageNumber=15.

Levine, Marianne. "McConnell won't allow vote on election reform bill," Mar. 6, 2019, Politico, https://www.politico.com/story/2019/03/06/mcconnell-election-reform-bill-1207702.

Lieberman, Hallie. "Was it Hershey or Reese That Made Peanut Butter Cups Great?" Atlas Obscura, Oct. 27, 2016. https://www.atlasobscura.com/articles/was-it-hershey-or-reese-that-made-peanut-butter-cups-great.

Liptak, Kevin, Alex Marquardt, Evan Perez, David Shortell, and Jeremy Diamond. "60 minutes of mayhem: How aggressive politics and policing turned a peaceful protest into a violent confrontation." CNN, June 2, 2020, https://www.cnn.com/2020/06/02/politics/trump-white-house-protest-police-church-photo-op/index.html.

Lockhart, P.R. "How Shelby County v. Holder upended voting rights in America. Vox, June 25, 2019. https://www.vox.com/policy-and-politics/2019/6/25/18701277/shelby-county-v-holder-anniversary-voting-rights-suppression-congress .

Lorch, Donatella. "Young Voters, Diverse and Disillusioned, Are Unpredictable in '96 Race." *New York Times*, Mar. 30, 1986. https://www.nytimes.com/1996/03/30/us/young-voters-diverse-and-disillusioned-are-unpredictable-in-96-race.html?searchResultPosition=1.

Mac Farquhar, Neil. "What's a Soccer Mom Anyway?" New York Times, Oct. 20, 1996. https://www.nytimes.com/1996/10/20/weekinreview/what-s-a-soccer-mom-anyway.html?searchResultPosition=8.

McCutcheon, Chuck. "Can White House hopefuls win over Millenials?" CQ Researcher, Oct. 2, 2015. https://library.cqpress.com/cqresearcher/document.php?id=cqresrre2015100200.

Mai-Duc, Christine. "Will billionaire Tom Steyer's big bet on young voters pay off in midterm election?" *Los Angeles Times*, Oct. 22, 2018. http://www.latimes.cbig bet on young votersom/politics/la-pol-ca-young-voters-midterms-20181022-story.html.

Mastrianni, Keia. "'Election Cake' Makes a Modern Day Resurgence." *Bon Appetit*, Oct. 17, 2016. https://www.bonappetit.com/entertaining-style/trends-news/article/election-cake-history .

McFadden, Robert D. "Wrapped in U.S. Flag, Madonna Raps for Vote," *New York Times*, Oct. 20, 1990 at 7. https://www.nytimes.com/1990/10/20/us/wrapped-in-us-flag-madonna-raps-for-vote.html .

Millstein, Seth. "The Average Age Of Congress In 2019 Will Drop Dramatically Thanks To Newly-Elected Millennials." Bustle, Nov. 9, 2018. https://www.bustle.com/p/the-average-age-of-congress-in-2019-will-drop-dramatically-thanks-to-newly-elected-millennials-13124359.

Nisbet, Mathew C. "A Look Back at 1992: How Bill Clinton Engaged Younger Voters." Dec. 13, 2011. Big Think. https://bigthink.com/age-of-engagement/a-look-back-at-1992-how-bill-clinton-engaged-younger-voters.

Paz, Isabella Grullon. "Democrats Seek Young Voters, and the Memes That Move Them." *New York Times*, Apr. 22, 2019. https://www.nytimes.com/2019/04/22/us/politics/youth-voters-2020.html?utm_source=Tisch+College+Contact+List&utm_campaign=263675b880-EMAIL_CAMPAIGN_2019_04_29_08_27&utm_medium=email&utm_term=0_246da4d028-263675b880-144249329.

People Staff. "The Eyes Have It in Idaho, Where Mr. Potato Head Is Running for Mayor of Boise." People, Nov. 4, 1985. https://people.com/archive/the-eyes-have-it-in-idaho-where-mr-potato-head-is-running-for-mayor-of-boise-vol-24-no-19/.

Peter, Jeremy W. and Yamiche Alcondor. "Hillary Clinton Struggles to Win Back Young Voters from Third Parties." New York Times, Sept. 28, 2016. https://www.nytimes.com/2016/09/29/us/politics/hillary-clinton-millennials-third-party.html?searchResultPosition=29.

Press, Joy. "Can MTV Use Peer Pressure to Get the Under-30 Crowd to Vote?" Vanity Fair, Oct. 30, 2018. https://www.vanityfair.com/hollywood/2018/10/mtv-launches-2018-midterm-elections-voting-campaign-aimed-at-post-millennials.

Rampell, Catherine. "Where are the young voters?" Washington Post, July 23, 2015. https://www.washingtonpost.com/opinions/where-are-the-young-voters/2015/07/23/2781990e-316f-11e5-8f36-18d1d501920d_story.html?utm_term=.dd5138c49d21.

Reed, Anika. "Taylor Swift teaches fans how to vote early in Instagram post." USA Today, Oct. 17, 2018. https://www.usatoday.com/story/life/people/2018/10/17/taylor-swift-teaches-fans-how-vote-early-instagram-post/1668622002/.

Reinhold, Robert. "A Portrait of Electorate: Large, Young and Reluctant." *New York Times*, Nov. 8, 1978, 18. https://timesmachine.nytimes.com/timesmachine/1978/11/08/112801673.html?pageNumber=18.

Roller, Emma. "I Registered to Vote...For This?". New York Times, Oct. 29, 2016. https://www.nytimes.com/2016/10/30/opinion/campaign-stops/i-registered-to-vote-for-this.html?searchResultPosition=1.

Roberts, Steven V. "Getting the Young Where They Live." *New York Times*, Sept. 29, 1986, B8. https://www.nytimes.com/1986/09/29/us/washington-talk-politics-getting-the-young-where-they-live.html?searchResultPosition=20.

Roberts, Steven V. "Younger Voters Tending to Give Reagan Support." *New York Times*, Oct. 16, 1984, 1 https://timesmachine.nytimes.com/timesmachine/1984/10/16/013754.html?pageNumber=1.

Rosenthal, Jack. "U.S. Voter Rolls Up By 13 Million." *New York Times*, Nov. 2, 1972, 1. https://timesmachine.nytimes.com/timesmachine/1972/11/02/79476752.html?pageNumber=1.

Rosenthal, Jack. "Youth Vote Held of Little Impact." *New York Times*, Jan. 4, 1973, 19. https://timesmachine.nytimes.com/timesmachine/1973/01/04/79830175.html?pageNumber=19.

Samuelsohn, Darren. "Obama's get-out-the-youth vote push." Politico, Oct. 27, 2012. https://www.politico.com/story/2012/10/the-obama-generation-x-factor-082959.

Saulny, Susan. "Scant Gains for Romney in a Poll of Young Voters." New York Times, Oct. 17, 2012. https://www.nytimes.com/2012/10/18/us/politics/polls-show-lost-opportunity-for-romney-among-young-voters.html?searchResultPosition=18.

Saulny, Susan. "Struggling Young Adults Are Question Mark for Campaigns." *New York Times*, Sept. 19, 2012. https://www.nytimes.com/2012/09/20/us/politics/struggling-young-adults-pose-challenge-for-campaigns.html?searchResultPosition=4.

Saulny, Susan. "Stung by Recession, Young Voters Shed Image as Obama Brigade." New York Times, July 1, 2012. https://www.nytimes.com/2012/07/02/us/politics/economy-cuts-into-obamas-youth-support.html?searchResultPosition=7.

Seelye, Katharine Q. "A Grand Old Party Animal Tries Courting Young Voters." *New York Times*, Jan. 21, 1996, 1. https://www.nytimes.com/1996/01/21/us/a-grand-old-party-animal-tries-courting-young-voters.html?searchResultPosition=5.

Southall, Ashley. "A 102-Year-Old Face of Voting Delays at the State of the Union." *New York Times*, Feb. 12, 2013. https://thecaucus.blogs.nytimes.com/2013/02/12/a-102-year-old-face-of-voting-delays-at-the-state-of-the-union/ .

Spillane, Ashley. "The state of the youth vote in America." MSNBC, Jan. 20, 2015. http://www.msnbc.com/msnbc/the-state-the-youth-vote-america.

Stephenson, Cassandra. "Election Day 2018: Meet the woman who signed the amendment allowing 18-year-olds to vote." *Jackson Sun*, Nov. 6, 2018. https://www.jacksonsun.com/story/news/local/2018/11/06/meet-woman-who-signed-amendment-allowing-18-year-olds-vote/1905213002/.

Stolberg, Sheryl Gay. "Young, Liberal and Open to Bog Government." New York Times, Feb. 10, 2013. https://www.nytimes.com/2013/02/11/us/politics/in-montana-young-liberal-and-open-to-big-government.html?searchResultPosition=1.

Stout, David. "The Campaign on Campus." *New York Times*, Nov. 3, 1996, 4. https://timesmachine.nytimes.com/timesmachine/1996/11/03/886092.html?pageNumber=183 .

Stradley, Linda. "Election Day Cake History and Recipe," https://whatscookingamerica.net/History/Cakes/ElectionCake.htm (accessed Jun. 29, 2020).

Strong, Robert A. "Jimmy Carter: Campaigns and Elections." Miller Center, University of Virginia. https://millercenter.org/president/carter/campaigns-and-elections.

Surdam, Maia. "Election Cake." AHA Today, Nov. 1, 2016 https://www.historians.org/publications-and-directories/perspectives-on-history/november-2016/election-cake-a-forgotten-democratic-tradition (accessed Jun. 29, 2020).

Suro, Roberto. "Democrats Court Youngest Voters." *New York Times*, Oct. 30, 1992, 18 https://www.nytimes.com/1992/10/30/us/the-1992-campaign-the-youth-vote-democrats-court-youngest-voters.html?searchResultPosition=4.

Toner, Robin. "Clinton Captures Presidency with Huge Electoral Margin." *New York Times*, Nov. 4, 1992, 1. https://www.nytimes.com/1992/11/04/us/1992-elections-president-overview-clinton-captures-presidency-with-huge.html?searchResultPosition=14.

Trussell, C.P. "Senate Defeats President's Plan For Voting at 18," May 22, 1954, *New York Times*, 1. https://timesmachine.nytimes.com/timesmachine/1954/05/22/issue.html.

Twombly, Matthew and Kendrick McDonald (research). "A Timeline of 1968: The Year the Shattered America." *Smithsonian Magazine*, Jan. 2018. https://www.smithsonianmag.com/history/timeline-seismic-180967503/.

United Press International. "Vote-at-18 Movement Spreading." Desert Sun, Jan. 11, 1969. https://cdnc.ucr.edu/?a=d&d=DS19690111.2.7&e=————en—20—1—txt-txIN————1 https://www.pacific.edu/Documents/marketing/review/40%20BIT_vF_Lrz.pdf.

Usborne, David. "Desilene Victor at 102 queued for six hours to vote for Obama. Now 106, she just early voted for Hillary Clinton." *Independent*, Nov. 7, 2016 https://www.independent.co.uk/news/world/americas/us-elections/desiline-victor-106-stood-in-line-barack-obama-hillary-clinton-miami-black-turnout-florida-a7401696.html .

Vena, Jocelyn. "Barack Obama Tells Youth Ball His 'Improbable Journey' Was 'Energized By Young People.'" MTV News, Jan. 20, 2009. http://www.mtv.com/news/1603129/barack-obama-tells-youth-ball-his-improbable-journey-was-energized-by-young-people/.

VI. Books and Journals

Amar, Akhil Reed. *America's Constitution: A Biography*. New York: Random House, 2006.

Amar, Akhil Reed. *America's Unwritten Constitution: The Precedents and Principles We Live By*. New York: Basic Books, 2012.

Appleby, Joyce, Eileen Chang, and Neva Goodwin, eds., *Encyclopedia of Women in American History, Volume 1, Colonization, Revolution, and the New Nation, 1585-1820*. Armonk, NY: Sharpe Reference, 2002.

Benton, Josiah Henry. *Voting in the Field: A Forgotten Chapter of the Civil War*. Boston: Privately Printed, 1915.

Carter, Nathan H. and William L. Stone. *Reports of the Proceedings and Debates of the Constitutional Convention of 1821, Assembled for the Purpose of Amending the Constitution of the State of New York*. Albany: E. and E. Hosford, 1821.

Cheng, Jenny Diamond. "How Eighteen-Year-Olds Got the Vote." (August 4, 2016). Available at SSRN: https://ssrn.com/abstract=2818730 or http://dx.doi.org/10.2139/ssrn.2818730.

Cheng, Jenny Diamond. "Uncovering the Twenty-Sixth Amendment." PhD diss., University of Michigan, 2008. https://deepblue.lib.umich.edu/bitstream/handle/2027.42/58431/jdiamond_1.pdf.

Cheng, Jenny Diamond. "Voting Rights for Millennials: Breathing New Life into the

Twenty-Sixth Amendment." *Syracuse Law Review* 67 (March 2017).

Cox, Archibald. "Foreword: Constitutional Adjudication and the Promotion of Human Rights." *Harvard Law Review* 80 (November 1966).

Cultice, Wendell. *Youth's Battle for the Ballot: A History of Voting Age in America*. New York: Greenwood Press, 1992.

De Schweinitz, Rebecca. "The Proper Age for Suffrage." In *Age in America: The Colonial Era to the Present*, edited by Corinne T. Field and Nicholas L. Syrett, 209-36. New York and London: New York University Press, 2015.

Engdahl, Sylvia. *Amendment XXVI: Lowering the Voting Age*. Farmington Hills, MI: Greenhaven Press, 2010.

Johnsen, Julia, ed. *Lowering the Voting Age*. New York: H.W. Wilson Co., 1944.

Keyssar, Alexander. *The Right to Vote: The Contested History of Democracy in the United States*. New York: Basic Books, 2000.

Lichtman, Alan. *The Embattled Vote in America: From the Founding to the Present*. Cambridge: Harvard University Press, 2020.

Mitchell, William C. *Why Vote?* Chicago: Markham Publishing Company, 1971.

Perry, Barbara A. *Edward M. Kennedy: An Oral History*. New York: Oxford University Press, 2019.

Seuss, Dr. Oh, *The Places You'll Go!* New York: Random House, 1990.

Simmons, Amelia. *American Cookery*. A Facsimile of the Second Edition Printed in Albany, 1796. Bedford, MA: Applewood Books, 1996. https://books.google.com/books?id=_6CggcPs3iQC&printsec=frontcover&source=gbs_ge_summary_r&cad=0#v=onepage&q&f=false .

Waldman, Michael. *The Fight to Vote*. New York: Simon & Schuster, 2017.

VI. Selected Websites

Center for Information and Research on Civic Learning and Engagement (CIRCLE) www.civicyouth.org

Election Protection coalition https://866ourvote.org

Harvard Kennedy School Institute of Politics. Harvard Youth Poll. https://iop.harvard.edu/youth-poll

Pew Research Center https://www.pewresearch.org/about/

U.S. Election Assistance Commissionhttps://www.eac.gov

Vote.gov https://vote.gov

ABOUT THE AUTHOR

Sheri J. Caplan is the author of *Petticoats and Pinstripes: Portraits of Women in Wall Street's History* (Praeger 2013; ISBN: 978-1-4408-0265-2). The book traces the contributions of women to American finance from colonial days to modern times and received the Bronze Medal in the women/minorities category of the 2014 Axiom Business Book Awards. The *Library Journal* called it "A great read for those interested in business, history, women's studies, and/or money" and *Choice* recommended it as "A useful addition to business and women's studies collections, and especially worthwhile reading for female students." Her other writing, including commentaries, articles, and reviews, has been published by various prominent media outlets and entities, including American National Biography, *American Banker*, and the German Historical Institute. She received her B.A. in history from Yale University and her J.D. from the University of Virginia School of Law.

Made in the USA
Middletown, DE
26 August 2020